# AUSTRALIAN POLICY HANDBOOK

'The authors know all about the real world, having been there and done that, and they remind the reader from time to time that things are not simple out there. However, their aim is to explain how policy should be made, and how a shrewd government will try to see that it is made, as nearly as possible . . . it is practical, but also scholarly in the best sense.'

*David Corbett,*
*Emeritus Professor, Flinders University of South Australia*

'An absolutely invaluable reference tool for those who work in public policy, who wish to influence the outcome of public policy debate, or who teach or study in the area.'

*Professor Bill Russell,*
*Monash University*

'The Handbook addresses the hands-on needs of public-sector officers, analysts and managers by drawing on insights, lessons and good practices from recent Australian experience. It also neatly incorporates concepts, models and critical perspectives drawn from the best academic analyses in Australia and overseas and can serve as an excellent text or resource for tertiary courses in public policy.'

*Professor Andrew Parkin,*
*Flinders University of South Australia*

# AUSTRALIAN POLICY HANDBOOK

Peter Bridgman and Glyn Davis

ALLEN & UNWIN

Copyright © Peter Bridgman and Glyn Davis 1998

All rights reserved. No part of this book may be reproduced or transmitted in any form or by any means, electronic or mechanical, including photocopying, recording or by any information storage and retrieval system, without prior permission in writing from the publisher.

First published in 1998 by
Allen & Unwin
9 Atchison Street
St Leonards NSW 2065 Australia
Phone:  (61 2) 9901 4088
Fax:      (61 2) 9906 2218
E-mail:  frontdesk@allen-unwin.com.au
Web:    http://www.allen-unwin.com.au

National Library of Australia
Cataloguing-in-Publication entry:

Bridgman, Peter, 1956– .
   Australian policy handbook.

   Bibliography.
   ISBN 1 86448 608 2.

   1. Political planning—Australia. 2. Australia—Politics and government. I. Davis, Glyn. II. Title.

320.60994

Set in 10/12 pt Palatino by Grand Design
Printed by Australian Print Group, Maryborough, Victoria

10 9 8 7 6 5 4 3 2 1

# Contents

| | |
|---|---|
| Preface | viii |
| Acknowledgements | ix |
| Glossary | x |
| Introduction: Why an *Australian Policy Handbook*? | 1 |

**1 Why Does Policy Matter?**     3
- *Policy as authoritative choice*     4
- *Policy as hypothesis*     5
- *Policy as objective*     6

**2 The Institutions of Public Policy**     8
- *The Australian system of government*     8
- *The executive*     9
- *Cabinet*     9
- *Public servants*     11
- *A map of government*     11
- *Government as politics*     13
- *Government as policy*     13
- *Government as administration*     14
- *Bringing the players together*     17
- *Coordination through routines*     19

**3 A Policy Cycle**     21
- *Alternatives to the policy cycle*     22
- *An Australian policy cycle*     24
- *The policy cycle and institutions*     26
- *Good process and good policy*     27

**4 Identifying Issues**     30
- *The policy agenda*     30
- *The agenda metaphor*     30
- *Issue drivers*     31
- *What issues make the agenda?*     34
- *Issue attention cycle*     35
- *Identifying issues*     36
- *Defining problems*     37

|  |  | *Wicked problems* | *37* |
|---|---|---|---|
|  |  | *Non-decisions* | *38* |
|  |  | *Issue identification skills* | *40* |
|  | **5** | **Policy Analysis** | **41** |
|  |  | *The purpose of policy analysis* | *42* |
|  |  | *Rationality* | *42* |
|  |  | *A sequence for policy analysis* | *43* |
|  |  | *The analyst's toolkit* | *49* |
|  |  | *Economic framework* | *49* |
|  |  | *Social framework* | *52* |
|  |  | *Environmental framework* | *52* |
|  |  | *Legal framework* | *53* |
|  |  | *Political analysis* | *54* |
|  |  | *Agreement: an analytic tool* | *54* |
|  |  | *Why analysis?* | *56* |
|  | **6** | **Policy Instruments** | **58** |
|  |  | *Classifying policy instruments* | *59* |
|  |  | *Australian policy instruments* | *60* |
|  |  | *Policy through advocacy* | *61* |
|  |  | *Policy through money* | *62* |
|  |  | *Policy through government action* | *63* |
|  |  | *Policy through law* | *64* |
|  |  | *Choosing a policy instrument* | *65* |
|  | **7** | **Consultation** | **66** |
|  |  | *The role of consultation* | *66* |
|  |  | *Different types of consultation* | *67* |
|  |  | *Consultation instruments* | *69* |
|  |  | *Designing a consultation process* | *73* |
|  |  | *Consultation* | *76* |
|  | **8** | **Coordination** | **77** |
|  |  | *An overall policy framework* | *78* |
|  |  | *Coordination routines* | *79* |
|  |  | *Central agencies* | *81* |
|  | **9** | **The Decision** | **90** |
|  |  | *Cabinet routines* | *91* |
|  |  | *What goes to cabinet?* | *94* |
|  |  | *Briefing ministers* | *96* |

|  |  |  |
|---|---|---|
|  | *Recording cabinet decisions* | *98* |
|  | *Executive council* | *99* |
|  | *Cabinet* | *100* |
|  | *Sample cover page for a cabinet submission* | *100* |
| **10** | **Implementation** | **103** |
|  | *Policy design includes implementation* | *103* |
|  | *Conditions for successful implementation* | *104* |
|  | *Implementation instruments* | *105* |
|  | *Implementation traps* | *107* |
|  | *Designing an implementation strategy* | *110* |
| **11** | **Evaluation** | **112** |
|  | *Evaluation and the policy cycle* | *113* |
|  | *Types of evaluation* | *114* |
|  | *Evaluation measures* | *116* |
|  | *Method* | *117* |
|  | *Findings* | *118* |
|  | *Evaluation* | *119* |
| **12** | **Managing the Policy Process** | **120** |
|  | *Procedural integrity* | *120* |
|  | *Roles and ethics* | *122* |
|  | *Planning projects* | *124* |
|  | *Timing* | *126* |
|  | *Management and the policy process* | *128* |
|  | *Organising for public policy* | *130* |
|  | *Professionals* | *131* |
|  | *Managing the policy process* | *131* |
| **13** | **Checklists for Policy Development** | **132** |
|  | *Policy objectives* | *135* |
|  | *Policy advice objectives* | *136* |
|  | *Managing the policy cycle* | *136* |
|  | *Policy cycle objectives* | *137* |
|  | **Appendix — Internet Resources for Public Policy** | **142** |
|  | **References** | **149** |
|  | **Index** | **153** |

# Preface

Much is changing in the public sector, yet the need for good policy advice remains. Even governments which contract out services still need expert advice about policy choices, and a professional approach to decision making.

While policy can never be reduced to rigid rules, this innovative *Australian Policy Handbook* provides an accessible, systematic and realistic approach to policy choices at all levels of government, leading to a better understanding of the requirements for good policy.

Using a policy cycle approach, the *Australian Policy Handbook* offers a path through the complexities of decision making and a simple, practical guide to each stage of the policy process.

The authors stress always the need to be open-minded about options, rigorous when assessing alternatives, and able to support recommendations with argument and evidence. The policy cycle described in these pages emphasises consultation within and beyond government, and evaluation to test objectives against outcomes.

Above all, the *Australian Policy Handbook* recognises the different roles of people involved with government. Some, such as public servants, offer expert and non-partisan advice, while ministers and their advisers bring a political eye to policy proposals. Brought together through the cabinet process, these roles offer complimentary skills and perspectives in the pursuit of good policy.

The *Australian Policy Handbook* will fill an important need for training material about the policy process. As National President of the Institute of Public Administration Australia, an organisation dedicated to advancing the practice and study of public administration, I welcome this initiative. It should provide for many an essential grounding in the basics of government decision making, and is an important contribution to better public policy.

*Dr Michael Keating AC*

*Dr Michael Keating is National President of the Institute of Public Administration Australia, a post he assumed on retiring as Secretary of the Department of Prime Minister and Cabinet in August 1996. He is a visiting Fellow in the Research School of Social Science at the Australian National University, and an Adjunct Professor with the Centre for Australian Public Sector Management at Griffith University.*

# Acknowledgements

The impetus for writing this *Australian Policy Handbook* arose from our experience working in government. Both authors noticed ever more frequent requests for policy training. The topic arose often — on senior management development courses, during performance appraisal sessions, in discussions sponsored by the Institute of Public Administration Australia (IPAA), and during the practical task of analysing and implementing policies.

Recent public sector change demands a greater range of skills from managers, including competence in policy formulation.

We hope the *Australian Policy Handbook* will help meet that need. Our publisher, John Iremonger, has encouraged us to reach out to a national audience interested in policy, and to provide a practical guide for action. His support is appreciated.

A number of colleagues, serving public servants and academics, provided comments and suggestions. We are deeply grateful for often very detailed textual comments from Susan Booth, Jacki Byrne, David Corbett, Margaret Gardner, Michael Keating, Jenny McDonald, Cynthia Newbown, David Newman, Michael Roche, Philip Selth, Ken Smith, R.F.I. Smith, John Wanna, Pat Weller and Howard Whitton. It is not their fault if we sometimes failed to heed good advice.

The layout for this volume was the responsibility of the talented Lyn Bennett and her fledgling company Grand Design. The development of new graphics was generously assisted by a small research grant from Griffith University. Important editorial and indexing assistance was provided by Terry Wood of the Centre for Australian Public Sector Management, and subediting by Susan Eggins.

Since Peter remains a public servant, he must remind readers the views expressed in this book are personal, and do not necessarily represent those of his employer, the State of Queensland.

Glyn, on the other hand, resigned his post as Director-General of the Queensland Office of the Cabinet some time ago for the splendours of academic inquiry, and is not so constrained. He would like, however, to express appreciation for the continuing Australia Research Council fellowship that allowed this work to proceed.

# Glossary

A common language is prerequisite to shared policy understanding. This Glossary is offered to facilitate that common language.

**act**
law made by parliament
*See also:* legislation
*Compare:* regulation

**administrator**
head of state for the Northern Territory
*See also:* head of state
*Compare:* governor; governor-general

**agency; government agency**
a department or other entity, usually formed under an act, that discharges government functions
*Compare:* department of state

**appropriations; annual appropriation**
1. acts that appropriate money for the government to spend on its activities. 2. parliament's authority to a government to spend monies from consolidated funds or loan funds for specified purposes
*See also:* budget

**assent; royal assent**
approval of a bill by the governor-general or governor, making it law. The final stage of parliament's legislative action, making a bill into an act
*See also:* commencement

**backbench**
1. members of parliament who are not ministers or shadow ministers, and who hold no other special office (e.g. speaker or president). 2. the seats at the back of a legislative chamber, occupied by those members
*See also:* members

**bicameral system**
a parliamentary system with two houses of parliament. The commonwealth and all state parliaments, with the exception of Queensland, are bicameral
*See also:* house of parliament
*Compare:* unicameral system

**bill**
proposed act introduced to parliament, but not yet passed and given assent
*See also:* assent
*Compare:* act; delegated legislation

**budget**
government's annual plan of revenue and expenditure. The budget is a major statement of policy intentions, and takes the form of appropriation bills, various budget statements and the treasurer's budget speech (the second reading speech on the appropriation bills)
*See also:* appropriations

**by-election**
an election to fill a seat left vacant because a member has resigned or died, or is otherwise ineligible to sit as a member
*Compare:* general election

**cabinet**
1. a group of senior ministers, responsible for a government's major policy decisions. In some states and the territories, all ministers are in the cabinet. 2. a meeting of ministers called as cabinet

**cabinet bag**
*See:* cabinet folder

**cabinet folder**
a collection of cabinet papers, delivered in an envelope and usually kept in a locked briefcase. The folder contains the agenda and submissions for a cabinet meeting

**cabinet submission**
a document prepared for cabinet's consideration on a policy matter

**central agency**
a department or office within a department responsible for policy, economic or personnel coordination across government
*Compare:* line department

**chamber**
the room in which a house of parliament meets

**chief minister**
the leader of a territory's government
*Compare:* prime minister; premier

**COAG**
Council of Australian Governments
*See also:* ministerial council

## commencement
the starting date for an act. Acts commence on assent, unless stated otherwise. The alternative is for the act to commence by a proclamation made by the executive council, usually done to allow other implementation to take place after the act is passed, such as subordinate legislation

## Commonwealth
1. the national entity of Australia, called 'the Commonwealth of Australia'. 2. the national level of government within the federation. 3. short name for the Commonwealth of Nations, mostly consisting of member states once British colonies
*See also: state; federation*

## confidence
1. the measure of the lower house of parliament's support for a government. Success of a motion of 'no confidence' or 'want of confidence' would normally result in a government resigning, and another government being formed or an election being called. 2. a measure of the support of a house of parliament in a minister

## conscience vote
vote in which members are not bound by party discipline, commonly used where issues of morality are debated, such as euthanasia or sexual preference

## constitution
1. the legal foundation of the nation, a state or territory, consiting of constitutional laws and practice. 2. the act of parliament that defines the role and power of the parliament

## cross the floor
to vote in parliament against party policy position

## crossbench
seats in the chamber occupied by independents or members of minor parties that form neither government nor opposition
*Compare: backbench; frontbench*

## crown
1. the Queen as head of state, represented by the governor-general for the Commonwealth and the governors for the states. 2. the legal entity of the Commonwealth or the states (as in 'the Crown in the right of the Commonwealth')
*See also: executive government*

## delegated legislation
*See: subordinate legislation*

## department of state; government department
organisational structure within government, staffed by public servants. Ministers are responsible for one or more departments, although a department may have several ministers, especially large Commonwealth departments

## discussion paper
document released by government seeking public comment on a matter, traditionally printed on green paper
*See also: green paper*
*Compare: policy paper; white paper*

## dissolution of parliament
termination of parliament by issue of writs for a general election. Usually called by the head of state on the advice of the leader of the government, or when a government loses parliament's confidence

## estimates
expenditure plans for departments or programs
*See also: budget*

## evaluation
a process for examining the worth of a program, by measuring outputs and outcomes, and comparing these with targets

## executive council
the body that advises the head of state in the discharge of the government's formal functions. Ministers are members of the executive council
*Compare: cabinet*

## executive government
that part of government concerned with policy choices and the delivery of public services, in contrast to the legislature and the judiciary
*See also: separation of powers*

## federation
1. the creation in 1901 of the Commonwealth of Australia from the colonies that became the states. 2. the federated states and the Commonwealth government
*See also: Commonwealth*

## franchise
the right to vote in an election

**frontbench**
1. the senior members of the government, being the ministers, and the opposition, the shadow ministers. 2. the seats at the front of a chamber, occupied by those members
*Compare: backbench; crossbench*

**general election**
an election for all members of the lower house
*Compare: by-election*

**government**
the party or parties in coalition that have the confidence of the lower house, and from whose number ministers are appointed
*Compare: opposition*

**government legislation**
bills prepared under authority of the government and introduced by a minister
*Compare: private member's bill*

**government of the day**
1. the executive branch of government. 2. the government holding office at any one time, used as such to describe government as a stable institution, independent from political notions of a party group winning power and becoming the government

**governor**
the Queen's representative in a state, and the head of state for that jurisdiction
*See also: administrator; governor-general; head of state*

**governor in council**
the executive council of a state
*See also: governor-general in council*

**governor-general**
the Queen's representative in Australia and head of state for the Commonwealth
*See also: administrator; governor-general; head of state*

**governor-general in council**
the executive council of the Commonwealth

**green paper**
a discussion paper, so called because it was at Westminster traditionally printed on green paper
*See also: discussion paper*

**Hansard**
written largely verbatim records of parliamentary debate
*Compare: votes and proceedings*

**head of government**
the prime minister of the Commonwealth, a premier of a state, and a chief minister for a territory
*See also: COAG*
*Compare: head of state*

**head of power**
authority in an act to make subordinate legislation or make a certain decision. If there is no head of power, the subordinate legislation or decision is unlawful

**head of state**
the Queen, represented in the Commonwealth by the governor-general, and in the states by governors
*See also: administrator; governor; governor-general*
*Compare: crown; head of government*

**house of assembly**
the lower house of parliament in South Australia and Tasmania
*See also: Legislative Assembly*

**house of parliament**
1. the building in which parliament meets. 2. each house in a bicameral system (e.g. House of Representatives and the Senate for the Commonwealth; Legislative Assembly and Legislative Council for most states) and the one house in a unicameral system (in Australia, the Legislative Assembly of the Australian Capital Territory, the Northern Territory and Queensland)
*See also: parliament*

**House of Representatives**
The lower house of the Commonwealth parliament

**leader of government business**
the member responsible for the conduct of the government's business through a house of parliament, usually a minister
*Compare: whip*

**leader of the opposition**
the leader of the party or group of parties forming the parliamentary opposition

**legislation**
law made by parliament, or by another person or body under a delegation by parliament
*See also: act; regulation; subordinate legislation*

**legislative assembly**
the lower house in the states. For Queensland and the territories, the only house of parliament

**legislative council**
the upper house in the states, except Queensland

**line department**
a department responsible for delivery of services to the community on behalf of executive government
*Compare:* central agency

**lobby**
1. the area immediately outside the chamber reserved for use by members, where they meet journalists, policy advisers or 'lobbyists'. 2. attempt to influence opinions or policy decisions of government

**lower house**
the house of parliament from which the government of the day derives. For the Commonwealth, the House of Representatives, and for the bicameral states, the legislative assembly or house of assembly
*See also:* bicameral

**machinery of government**
the structure of executive government departments, determined by the head of the government in allocating portfolio responsibilities to ministers

**mandate**
support claimed by a government for its policies from its most recent electoral victory

**member; MHA; MHR; MLA; MLC; MP**
1. a person elected to a seat in a house of parliament. 2. a member of a lower house: MHR for Member of the House of Representatives; MHA for Member of the House of Assembly (South Australia and Tasmania); MLA for Member of the Legislative Assembly; MLC for Member of the Legislative Council. Some members use MP for Member of Parliament

**minister**
a member of the government responsible for administering a portfolio, including the prime minister, premier and chief minister of a jurisdiction. Ministers are members of the executive council. The cabinet is made up of ministers
*See also:* ministerial responsibility; responsible government

**ministerial council**
a meeting of Commonwealth, state and territory ministers responsible for a certain policy area. New Zealand and Papua New Guinea's ministers sometimes participate
*See also:* COAG

**ministerial responsibility**
a doctrine that holds ministers responsible for their government's policies and for the actions of public servants in their departments
*See also:* responsible government; Westminster system

**natural justice**
legal rules requiring decision makers to act fairly and in good faith, without bias (pre-judgement or interest in a matter), to provide details of any matters affecting individuals and to ensure a fair hearing

**non-government legislation**
*See:* private member's bill
*Compare:* government legislation

**opposition**
the main political party or coalition of parties that is not the government
*Compare:* government

**order in council**
a form of subordinate legislation made by executive council
*See also:* subordinate legislation

**parliament**
1. the legislative arm of government. For the Commonwealth, the Queen, represented by the governor-general, the Senate and the House of Representatives. Generally, the head of state and each house of parliament. 2. the period between general elections (for example the 15th Commonwealth Parliament, from 1937 to 1940)

**parliamentary committee**
a group of members assigned a task of investigating and reporting to the parliament or a house of parliament on a particular matter

**parliamentary counsel**
specialists in drafting legislation

**peak body**
pressure group representing interests of many other groups with related interests
*See also:* lobby; pressure group

**plain English**
content, language, presentation, structure and style aimed at making material readable and understandable by the target audience for the material. Often contrasted with legalese. Also contrasted simply with poorly written material

**platform**
the electoral undertakings of a political party

**policy analysis**
1. analysis of a policy problem, designed to state the nature of the problem, leading to options for addressing the issue. 2. analysis of government's action, designed to discern the underlying policy choices of that government

**policy instrument**
the means by which a policy is put into effect

**policy paper**
statement of a government's policy intention in a particular area. Also called a 'white paper' because it is traditionally printed on white bond paper
*Compare: discussion paper, green paper*

**policy professional**
an adviser with expertise and skills in a substantive policy area. As with 'policy analyst', the term is used only rarely in Australia

**portfolio**
the responsibilities of a minister, made up of the acts the minister administers, the organisations accountable to the minister and other functions of the minister. Portfolios are assigned by the prime minister, premier or chief minister

**premier**
the leader of a state government
*Compare: prime minister; chief minister*

**president**
the presiding officer of the Senate
*Compare: speaker*

**pressure group**
group that attempts to influence opinions or decisions of government or opposition without themselves seeking election to parliament
*See also: lobby*

**prime minister**
the leader of the Commonwealth government
*Compare: chief minister; premier*

**private member's bill**
a bill introduced by a member other than a minister
*Compare: government legislation*

**prorogation**
termination of a parliamentary session by the governor-general or governor without a general election
*Compare: dissolution of parliament*

**public policy**
1. intentions and deeds of a government. 2. description of principles governing the way decisions are made

**public servant**
employee of government under a public service act, usually in a department of government. Compare employees in statutory authorities, or employed under specific acts, such as police officers

**regulation**
form of subordinate legislation made by executive council, usually describing detailed administrative or technical matters

**representative government**
form of government in which franchise holders elect a person to represent their interests in parliament

**reserve powers**
powers reserved to the head of state, including, for example, power to dismiss a government

**responsible government**
system of government in which the executive must be supported by parliament, and answerable to the people through an electoral process. Sometimes called the Westminster system, reflecting its origins in the British parliament located in the Palace of Westminster
*See also: representative government*

**retrospective operation**
application of laws before the day the law comes into effect, a device usually considered repugnant because people cannot obey a law that did not exist at the relevant time. Sometimes used to implement taxation changes from the date the policy was announced to prevent tax avoidance in the interim

**royal assent**
*See:* assent

**SCAG**
Standing Committee of Attorneys-General, a ministerial committee

## second reading speech
speech made by the member introducing a bill into parliament, stating the policy of the bill. These speeches are admissible evidence in court of the intention of the law. For government legislation, this speech is made by the relevant minister

## Senate
The upper house of the Commonwealth parliament
*Compare: House of Representatives*

## senator
a member of the Senate
*Compare: member*

## separation of powers
doctrine holding that the legislative, judicial and executive arms of government should be separate and, in particular, that the executive should not seek to direct the work of the judiciary or to misuse for political purposes the discretionary authority of the police service

## shadow cabinet
meeting of shadow ministers

## shadow minister
member of the opposition responsible for nominated policy area, and said to 'shadow' the relevant minister

## speaker
the presiding officer of the lower house of parliament

## standing orders
rules about the conduct of debate and business in a house of parliament

## state
1. the legal entity of a nation at international law (for Australia, the Commonwealth of Australia). 2. one of the six states within the federation. 3. the legal entity of a jurisdiction (e.g. Commonwealth of Australia; state of New South Wales; Australian Capital Territory). 4. geographical area of one of the six states. 5. the body politic
*See also: Commonwealth; federation; territory*

## statutory authority
an agency of the government, created under an act
*Compare: department of state*

## subordinate legislation
legislation made under an act, by a person other than parliament. Regulations, made by executive council, are the most common. Also called delegated legislation because it is made under parliament's delegation

## supply
budget allocation that allows government to fund its programs, including salaries to public servants
*See also: appropriations; budget*

## territory
Australian Capital Territory and Northern Territory, each of which has self-government under Commonwealth acts as opposed to the constitution
*Compare: state*

## unicameral system
A parliamentary system with one house of parliament. This system prevails in Queensland and the territories. New Zealand's parliament is also unicameral

## uniform legislation
legislation that applies uniformly throughout the federation because each jurisdiction has made or adopted the law. Compare Commonwealth legislation that applies throughout the federation and overrides any incompatible state or territory law

## upper house
one of two houses in bicameral systems. The Senate for the Commonwealth; the legislative council for a state
*Compare: lower house*

## votes and proceedings
official record of parliamentary business
*See also: Hansard*

## Westminster system
*See: responsible government*

## whip
the member of a party responsible for keeping the party members informed about parliament's business, especially if a vote is expected. The whip and deputy whip are usually not ministers
*Compare: leader of government business*

## white paper
*See: policy paper*
*Compare: discussion paper*

# Introduction

# Why an *Australian Policy Handbook?*

We shape our world through public policy.

This public policy is made not only by politicians, but by thousands of public servants and the tens of thousands of women and men who petition parliaments and ministers, who join interest groups, comment through the media or represent unions, corporations and community movements. All have a stake in public policy.

Public policy draws people, institutions, markets and governments into the familiar patterns of decision making. This necessarily means that settling and administering policy is complex, because many players influence the choices made.

Preparing a viable policy proposal can be a daunting task, requiring intense activity and coordination with other government decisions to ensure consistency. The process is long and often convoluted, as decision makers weigh up expert evidence, political and bureaucratic advice, and the competing interests of those affected by the policy proposal. Finding a way through the policy maze can seem impossible.

There are, however, clues to guide us and skills that can be practised; despite appearances, policy processes generally follow a logic, a system. That system seeks to structure the way problems are understood and presented, so that decision makers can —

- hear about issues
- understand options
- learn of informed opinion
- make choices
- test their decisions.

In this *Australian Policy Handbook* we suggest a model to describe this system, a *cycle* depicting the rhythms and patterns of the policy world. This is a tool to illustrate the regular sequence of steps involved in decision making. The

> **Snapshot**
> This *Australian Policy Handbook* is designed for those who become embroiled in the sometimes turbulent world of public policy, midway between politics and public administration.
>
> They range from senior advisers and executives to technical advisers and support staff.
>
> Standing outside the process looking in are the students of politics and policy, and interest groups keen to influence policy choices. They too might find something of interest in these pages.

> The *Australian Policy Handbook* offers one view of the policy process and suggestions about each step. It is designed to be pragmatic and accessible, of immediate use to practitioners, clients and those who observe.
>
> We aspire to best practice in public policy, but recognise the constraints on all who enter the maze. The cycle identified in these pages is by no means the only way to make sense of policy making, but it is a systematic approach that can bring a consistent set of actions to each policy issue.

policy cycle is used to identify a need, explore possible responses, apply the resources and expertise of government and, finally, to test if the desired outcome has been achieved.

To some, the idea of a policy handbook might seem misguided; policy is the artistic pinnacle of political enterprise. A handbook would be painting by numbers.

We recognise the complexity and discretionary nature of policy decision making, but we also believe strongly that good process can help create better policy. By process we do not mean something mechanical or standardised; policy is too much shaped by the particular problem it addresses and by a rich constellation of laws, budgets, and political circumstance to be reduced to immutable rules.

However there *are* constants in good policy making — an intellectual rigour about issues, a commitment to procedural integrity, and a willingness to experiment and learn through implementation and adaptation. Policies are theories about the world; some flourish while others wither. The better designed the theory, the more tested its assumptions, the greater the chances for success. Process helps better design and more rigorous testing, but it is never a substitute for them.

We discuss policy making in an Australian context, since local institutions and traditions help order how choices are reached. Because national and state governments in Australia rely on similar policy structures and routines, it should be possible to describe a process that holds across this country. Variations across jurisdictions seem less important to us than shared Australian assumptions about how to make public policy. Readers can substitute their particular for our general.

A policy cycle is something of an ideal — worth striving for, if not always attainable. Good process is the foundation for good policy, even though the world does not always allow sufficient time for the careful, sequential, policy cycle discussed in these pages. It is important to be realistic yet strive for the best possible policy outcomes. This *Australian Policy Handbook* is a contribution to that endeavour.

# Chapter 1
# Why Does Policy Matter?

Through public policy, politicians make a difference. Policy is the instrument of governance, the decision that directs public resources in one direction but not another. It is the outcome of the competition between ideas, interests and ideologies that impels our political system.

There have been many attempts to define 'public policy', yet its meaning and boundaries remain ambiguous. Some policy documents and pronouncements are clearly expressions of public policy. Others are of uncertain status. For example —

- legislation states policy
- a white paper states the policy intentions of the government, yet these may not be realised
- a ministerial statement might be policy, but it might equally be one view on the way to the government forming a position
- election platforms describe a political party's intentions, but do they state the policy of the resulting government?
- is it 'policy' when government activities proceed without explicit statement of intent, continuing from government to government, never exciting public interest or political scrutiny?

We can agree policy is important without being certain we always mean the same thing. Hal Colebatch (1993) has explored the many definitions offered for 'public policy'. Often, policy is no more than 'whatever governments choose to do or not to do'. Sometimes we use the term to describe very specific choices, but the notion also embraces general directions and philosophies. There are also times 'policy' becomes clear only in retrospect; we look back and discern the patterns and continuities of a set of choices, and call these 'policy'. This multitude of meanings is inevitable, since

> **Snapshot**
> 'Public policy' is inherently difficult to define, but can be described by some of its characteristics.
>
> Public policy—
> - is intentional, designed to achieve a stated or understood purpose
> - involves decisions, and their consequences
> - is structured and orderly
> - is political in nature
> - is dynamic.
>
> This chapter sees public policy as an authoritative statement by a government about its intentions. It also views public policy as relying on hypotheses about cause and effect, and as structured around objectives.

policy is a shorthand description for everything from an analysis of past decisions to the imposition of current political thinking.

This chapter describes policy in three different but compatible ways. First, policy can be the *authoritative choice* of a government. Second, policy is a *hypothesis*, an expression of theories about cause and effect. Finally, policy is explored as the *objective* of governmental action.

## Policy as authoritative choice

Public policy emerges from the world of politics. This can be a chaotic place in which ideas must find a path between the intentions of politicians, the interests of various government institutions, the interpretations of bureaucrats and the intervention of pressure groups, media and citizens.

Central to this political world is the executive, that group of ministers around the leader, who exercise the authority of government on behalf of the parliament. Ministers understand the political nature of their work, but they also appreciate that other players need authoritative statements of policy direction. Power is exercised through the ability to issue directives and decisions expressing intention. Through policies, governments make their mark. From the chaos of politics must emerge the certainty of action.

Policy, then, can be seen as an authoritative response to a public issue or problem. This suggests that public policy —

- is *intentional*; public policy means pursuing specific government goals through the application of identified public or private resources
- is about *making decisions* and testing their consequences
- is *structured*, with identifiable players and a recognisable sequence of steps
- is *political* in nature, expressing the electoral and program priorities of the executive.

Policies reached through a decision making framework —

- express a considered response to a policy issue
- help shape a government's philosophy
- are an authoritative framework of the government's beliefs and intentions in the policy area.

Policy decisions are authoritative because they are made by people with legitimate power in our system of government.

> Public policy is 'deciding at any time and place what objectives and substantive measures should be chosen in order to deal with a particular problem, issue or innovation'.
> Dimock et al. in Hal Colebatch, 1993:33

These decisions might bind public servants to act in a particular way, or direct future action such as preparing legislation for parliament's consideration.

Despite being authoritative, decisions may not be realised. The slip between hope and outcome is all too familiar. Nor does the authoritative nature of public policy mean that government has deliberated on every issue. Each government must work from the legacy of its predecessors. Comfortable bureaucratic routines often reflect an ancient policy decision. Still, a well developed policy process ensures that intentions are regularly considered and examined against results.

## Policy as hypothesis

Policies are built on theories about the world, models of cause and effect. Policies must make assumptions about behaviour. They contain incentives that encourage one behaviour over another, or disincentives to discourage particular actions. Policies must incorporate guesses about compliance, and mechanisms to deal with shirking, to enforce compliance.

But public policy is not a laboratory experiment, and it is difficult to test behavioural assumptions before a policy is implemented. Cabinet might, for example, judge that a package of taxation measures will elicit a desired response from the citizens. Until the government announces the tax and measures its effects, ministers remain unsure if they have correctly identified cause and effect in the tax system.

Policy is created amid uncertainty, and tested in the most demanding of circumstances. Policy makers learn by finding and correcting errors in policy assumptions and design.

For example, in 1996 the Howard government implemented an incentive scheme to encourage greater participation in private health insurance. It was assumed the rebate would encourage individuals to behave in a particular way — to take out private health insurance.

Yet almost immediately the incentive was put in place, private health insurers announced premium increases equal to the rebate. Cabinet may have correctly judged the behavioural incentives for consumers, but it appeared suprised by the response of another key group. Government's challenge then is to learn from this outcome, and build a different policy model.

> ... public policy is the complex interplay of values, interests and resources. Policies express values, support or curtail interests and distribute resources. They shape, and are shaped by, the constituent elements of politics, so that policies represent victories or compromises encapsulated as programs for action by government.
>
> Glyn Davis et al., 1993:4

**Public policy versus Private policy**
Public policy is a course of action by government designed to attain specific results. Non-government organisations have policies too, but they cannot call on public resources or legal coercion in the same way.

> Policy can be seen as —
> - a label for a field of activity
> - an expression of general purpose or desired state of affairs
> - specific proposals (e.g. by interest groups, cabinet)
> - decisions of government (arising from crucial moments of choice)
> - formal authorisation — a specific act or statute
> - a program — a particular package of legislation or administrative arrangements, organisation and resources
> - output — what government actually delivers, as opposed to what it has promised or has authorised through legislation
> - the product of a particular activity
> - theory — if we do X, then Y will follow
> - a process unfolding over a long period of time.
>
> drawn from Brian Hogwood and Lewis Gunn, 1990:13–19

Good policy processes will make behavioural assumptions explicit, so that decision makers understand the model of the world that supports a recommendation. To think of policy as hypothesis puts into words the mental calculations that guide all policy advisers and makers.

The notion of policy as hypothesis also stresses the importance of learning from policy implementation and evaluation. Good policy making assumes an ability to draw lessons from policy experience and to apply that information in the next spin of the policy cycle. Given the multiple players in policy making, and often drawn-out processes, incorporating policy learning can be difficult. Hence the need for a structured policy process, so that learning is documented and passed on.

As American policy analyst Aaron Wildavsky (1987:393) observed, 'we hope that new hypotheses expand into theories that better explain the world'. These better theories, guided by the results of evaluation, become the basis for improved public policies.

## Policy as objective

Public policy is ultimately about achieving objectives. It is a means to an end. Policy is a course of action by government designed to attain certain results.

The policy process must help decision makers clarify their objectives. A policy without purpose serves no purpose, and may do a great deal of harm. When policies that lack point or coordination take effect, programs begin to draw in different directions, the overall strategy disappears, and commentators soon speak of a government 'losing its way'.

Good policy advice avoids this trap by making explicit —
- the form of authoritative statement required
- the model of cause and effect underpinning the policy
- the goals to be achieved.

As later chapters illustrate, an effective policy cycle checks a particular policy proposal against the broader objectives of government. Through consultation and interaction, the policy cycle encourages consistency, so a new policy will fit into the wider picture of government activity. Public policy is made by many people, in a chain of choices that includes analysis, implementation, evaluation and reconsideration.

This coordination is only possible, though, if policy objectives are stated clearly and honestly. When intentions are uncertain or contradictory, a policy has little chance of success. Setting an objective is the first step in a long process. It is also the most important since only an objective can give point and reason to a public policy choice.

It is easy to lose sight of policy objectives. The 'solution' may become more important than the problem. Policy activity is very fast moving; once a decision is made, work gathers momentum. Time and authority to reflect on the chosen direction are limited, allowing a poor decision to cascade into a policy far removed from the original intention.

Often objectives are overtaken by unintended consequences — side effects discovered only after the policy is implemented, which undermine the policy's effect or create new, complex problems. A scheme to licence a particular activity can create a powerful elite, strongly wedded to the policy and so politically influential that later modification becomes costly and difficult. Taxation relief may distort the market for goods or services other than those originally targeted.

To keep policies focused on objectives, policy makers rely on a policy cycle that includes project planning and evaluation. Along the way they are likely to ask —

- what is the purpose of the policy?
- how will it affect
    - overall government direction
    - the department
    - client groups
    - interest groups
    - society?
- what is the relationship between the means of implementation and the policy objectives?
- how will this policy relate to other government objectives?
- can it make a difference in the ways intended?

Through a systematic policy cycle, decision makers seek an authoritative choice, based on a plausible hypothesis, that can deliver required outcomes. This deceptively simple formula sums up the challenge of good public policy.

# Chapter 2
# The Institutions of Public Policy

> **Snapshot**
>
> Public policy cannot be separated from its institutional context. Policy is essentially an expression of the political will of a government.
>
> So for policy professionals and for partisan participants alike, an understanding of the nature of government and the political dynamic is crucial.
>
> In this chapter, the traditional hierarchical theory of responsible government is complemented by a functional division of government into political, policy and administrative roles.

Policy is the means governments use to pursue their objectives. A statement of public policy is therefore a statement of political priorities. In the Australian system of government, though, not all actors involved in policy formulation are political. Indeed, much policy advice is prepared by public servants committed to notions of professional neutrality. The system must find ways to mesh such impartial expert advice with a political perspective.

This chapter sketches the institutional context of policy making. It offers both the formal model of the Australian political system — usually described as 'responsible government' — and a more dynamic representation of the interaction between politicians, advisers and the public service.

## The Australian system of government

The Australian system of government melds notions of ministerial responsibility, drawn from the House of Commons in the Palace of Westminster in London, with a federal Senate modelled on American practice. It includes a governor-general, as representative of the Queen, and a powerful executive that reflects party domination of the parliament. This unique system, given national expression in the Commonwealth Constitution of 1900, combines parliamentary government with federal institutions.

Australian governments gain their authority through the electoral process. A compulsory universal franchise makes voting a civic privilege and a duty for all adults. The people elect representatives to serve in the parliament, and to exercise power on their behalf.

By tradition, a system of responsible government has three main activities —

- legislative, or the making of laws; a power exercised by the parliament

- executive, or the administration and enforcement of the law, and the management of the resources of government. This function is carried out by ministers and the administrative agencies of government such as departments and statutory authorities
- judicial, the application and interpretation of the law to particular cases; a function of the courts.

The responsible government system allows for some overlap between these roles. Ministers are also members of parliament. Parliament delegates some law-making power to the executive. The judiciary, though, comprises independent judges who value highly their separation from political decision making.

## The executive

The principal focus of this *Australian Policy Handbook* is the executive arm of government. The various Australian, state and territory constitutions vest formal authority in executive council. However, the governor-general, governor or administrator is only a symbolic repository of power. The real authority of government is exercised by cabinet.

The principles of responsible government make parliament paramount. The executive must comply with parliament's wishes, expressed as legislation. Parliament can and does amend proposals made by the government, and monitors executive activity through an extensive committee system. The executive will fall if it loses the confidence of the lower house. In practical terms, though, the executive controls the legislative program of the parliament. Ministers hold office because they are part of a majority in the lower house.

The executive arm of government is the ministers, who each take responsibility for the policy directions of government departments and agencies under their supervision. Ministers must account to parliament for their stewardship of public service functions. Short of personal impropriety, resignations for poor administration are exceedingly rare in Australia.

## Cabinet

The cabinet is a meeting of ministers, chaired by the prime minister, premier or chief minister, at which political and policy decisions are made. Not all ministers necessarily sit in cabinet; the Commonwealth cabinet comprises only the

---

Hugh Emy and Owen Hughes (1991:338–39) identify five key components of Australian responsible government —

- formal constitutional authority is vested in the governor-general, as the Queen's representative
- in practice, executive authority is exercised by ministers individually and collectively. They meet as a cabinet to make choices on policy issues
- the executive can be dismissed from office by losing an election, or by losing a confidence vote in the House of Representatives. The Senate may block supply, depriving the government of sufficient money to continue its programs
- the executive is advised by a career public service, committed to serving 'without fear or favour'. The public service advises but does not govern; final decisions are the prerogative of ministers
- the system is kept honest and open by a direct accountability link 'running from officials to a minister and so to cabinet; then from ministers and cabinet to parliament, and from parliament and the cabinet to the electorate'.

In practice, of course, 'things are a good deal more complicated'.

> The Australian form of government is an innovation, drawing on Australian colonial traditions, British concepts of responsible government and American models of federalism. The result is captured in a written constitution and the surrounding constitutional conventions, the major features of which are a federal division of powers, a strong parliament, a separate Australian judiciary which reviews the constitutional validity of legislation, and an Australian representative of the monarch who exercises nearly all his or her functions on the advice of the executive and who performs the national ceremonial role normally associated with a head of state.
> Republic Advisory Committee, 1993:38

> **Cabinet composition**
> It is the prime minister who decides on the size of the cabinet and who determines which ministers are to be included in the cabinet.
> John Howard, 1990:4

most senior ministers. State and territory cabinets usually include all ministers.

Cabinet is the apex of government, the institution that must consider political, policy and administrative implications of any proposition, and settle a government position. Though a body without formal legal standing (the cabinet is not mentioned in the Commonwealth Constitution), it is the source for an authoritative allocation of government resources.

Patrick Weller (1990:33) argues that cabinet performs at least six major roles —

- cabinet as a *clearing-house* — across government, committees meet and choices are reached that require ratification. Cabinet acts as a clearing-house for this activity. Including a matter on the cabinet agenda makes all ministers aware of issues that may have been handled by a small committee, and provides an authoritative decision on an issue

- cabinet as an *information exchange* — government is so complex ministers can find it difficult to see beyond their own portfolio role. Weekly meetings of cabinet ensure ministers see the broader picture, and know what their colleagues are doing

- cabinet as *arbiter* — when government agencies disagree, cabinet provides a forum for resolution. More generally, cabinet arbitrates the inevitable tensions over resources and priorities that every government must address. This role is particularly important in the annual budget process, when agencies and programs compete for limited resources

- cabinet as *political decision maker* — though signed by ministers, most submissions put before cabinet are written by public servants. Cabinet must cast a political eye over policy proposals, asking about the electoral consequences of a course of action

- cabinet as *coordinator* — since agency responsibilities often overlap, policies that contradict initiatives elsewhere in government may arise. Cabinet is the only institution that can impose a coherent overall direction for government, by ensuring coordination of policies

- cabinet as *guardian of the strategy* — a government needs to set overall themes and objectives for its term in office, yet ministers can quickly become locked into a departmental perspective, seeing all issues from the narrow view of their own policy concerns. Cabinet is the forum that balances the particular with the general, so encouraging ministers to see issues from a 'whole of government' viewpoint.

In performing these multiple roles, cabinet often relies on the chair. It is the prime minister who must look to the overall strategy, and weigh the benefits of a proposal against the goals of the government. There is no 'rational calculus' guiding cabinet in many of its choices, only a willingness to think through all the implications of a submission and judge which course of action is best for the government and for the polity.

Ministers are assigned responsibility for certain organisational structures of government, the departments and agencies, and for administration of various acts, regulations and orders of parliament. The acts and organisations listed in the Administrative Arrangements Order make up the minister's portfolio. Each minister at the cabinet table represents portfolio concerns, and presents the portfolio's proposals for consideration.

> Prime ministers must work with their ministerial colleagues and through the institution of cabinet. In Australia, executive government is collective in its form and its expectations. The influence of the prime ministers and their impact on policy will depend on their capacity to cajole, persuade or bully cabinet colleagues — either individually or collectively — into accepting their approach or their solutions.
> Patrick Weller, 1992:5

## Public servants

Public servants are part of the executive arm of government. Not all public service work is directly concerned with policy development, but all public service endeavour is affected by public policy. The work of public servants is driven by the policy priorities of the government of the day.

Thus service delivery, administration and policy advice are integrated to the work of government and its political direction. In the ideal responsible government system, public servants advise governments on policy but do not become involved in direct political questions. These are the prerogative of the cabinet and of parliament. Ministers make decisions, while public servants offer advice and then implement government choices.

## A map of government

This standard picture of responsible government offers a chain of accountability. Public servants answer to ministers, ministers to parliament, parliament to the people. Some institutions, though, do not fit into this simple scheme. The courts can override the executive in some issues yet are not accountable to the people. Further complications arise from

> **Portfolio ministers**
> The prime minister sets out his priorities and strategic direction for each portfolio in a letter sent to respective ministers shortly after they are appointed. This letter may also indicate in broad terms how the prime minister sees functions being shared by ministers in the portfolio.
> John Howard, 1997:3

administrative law, with its accountability measures outside the standard information chain. Still, the familiar institutions of parliament, the executive, the public service and the courts are usefully defined and linked by the responsible government model.

There are other ways to look at the players within Australian government. A functional approach, for example, sets hierarchical notions aside and considers government from the perspective of three key coordination tasks (drawn from Davis, 1996:19) —

- *politics* — in a parliamentary system, governments must be seen to be united and coherent, to speak with one voice. Such consistency is an important political virtue, portraying a shared philosophy and shared goals. Politics is not only about implementing party platform; it also involves attaining and keeping government through policies that attract voters. While philosophy and ideology are important, pragmatic politics will pervade every government's judgements about the consequences of its decisions

- *policy* — a government stands or falls on its policy choices. It must ensure sufficient coordination so that one policy does not undermine another. Governments need to develop and monitor policy, and to achieve consistency across the many agencies which make up a modern public sector. The formulation of public policy is thus a key government task

- *administration* — policies mean nothing without a capacity to implement government decisions. Typically this means relying on the public servants or contractors who work for government. Ministers are accountable for efficient, effective and honest administration, and answer for the programs in their care.

Some overlap is inevitable between these functions. Ministers perform political roles, but are also involved in policy development and administration. Public servants are principally focused on policy advice and administration, but must also be sensitive to the political circumstances of their ministers. Viewing the political system in terms of political, policy and administrative tasks helps separate roles while providing some sense of the interplay between governmental players. The following sections outline each

> Politics inevitably intrudes into policy formulation because the instruments of power — information, resources and authority — are not centralised in the hands of a minister but fragmented across parties, departments, community groups and clients. Policy is therefore difficult to impose; it must be negotiated.
> 
> Glyn Davis and Patrick Weller, 1987:386

of these roles, and its characteristic participants, in more detail.

## Government as politics

Walk around Parliament House in Canberra and the intense activity is hard to miss. Parliament is the centre of a political world, the place where ministers put in long hours governing while their opposition numbers plot and scheme to bring them down. Around the politicians are their advisers, partisan figures hired to assist with political strategy and media presentation. Many also develop significant policy expertise in their own right, and offer ministers alternative political views about appropriate courses of action. While the public service tradition endures from one government to the next, advisers hold office only while their patron prospers. Their term may be very influential but short lived.

At the centre of the political world is the office of the leader — a prime minister in Canberra, a premier or chief minister in the states and territories. In a parliamentary setting, prime ministers are powerful but not presidential; they are still subject to the party in power, and can be removed from office by their own side at any time. Prime ministers must offer effective and strong leadership, while maintaining party room support. The standard test is electability — leaders who seem likely to win the next election can usually carry their colleagues in any challenge.

Leaders matter because they provide a public identity for a government, and a sense of coherence and direction. Leaders play a political role, but they are also the point at which politics must be married with policy and administration. While advisers are largely confined to the political world, prime ministers must reach beyond the confines of Parliament House to engage the broader agenda of public policy.

## Government as policy

When politicians become ministers, they assume responsibility for public policy outcomes. This requires ministers to work together as a cabinet in setting goals for the government. Policy duties also bring ministers into regular contact with the public service, and so into a world wider than politics.

At the centre of the policy system is cabinet, with its multiple roles and never ending workload. To manage cabinet

> The sheer complexity of government makes it hard for decision makers, especially ministers, to do their job effectively. There is so much to be read and understood. This does not just include the paperwork associated with the portfolio and cabinet. It includes newspapers, journals and the wide world of books. It has been observed that men and women who do not read are not fit to govern, yet ministers and chief executives rarely have time to do so.
>
> David Newman

> The Commonwealth and most states have a cabinet handbook which regulates what issues come to cabinet, and how submissions must be structured.
>
> The Commonwealth *Cabinet Handbook* imposes a maximum of seven pages for any cabinet submission. It requires submissions be lodged 10 days prior to consideration, and include details of consultation within and beyond government.
>
> Matters required to come before cabinet include —
>
> - new policy proposals and proposed significant variations to existing policies
> - proposals likely to have a significant effect on employment in either the public or private sector
> - expenditure proposals (normally only considered in a budget context)
> - proposals requiring legislation
> - proposals likely to have a considerable impact upon relations between the Commonwealth and foreign, state or local governments.
>
> Cabinet rules establish and give shape to the policy cycle, since cabinet submissions must include detail about issue identification, policy analysis, appropriate policy instruments, consultation, coordination, implementation and evaluation.

business, including the huge paper flow involved in circulating submissions and decisions, governments rely on a central policy agency. In Canberra this is the Department of the Prime Minister and Cabinet (PM&C), and in many states a department of the premier and cabinet or an office of the cabinet. As well as handling the logistics of cabinet meetings, PM&C provides the prime minister, as chair of cabinet, with a detailed briefing on all submissions (Walter, 1992). This ensures the prime minister has a comprehensive set of briefing notes on government business and can interrogate any minister about the detail of a submission. Officials from PM&C also sit in on cabinet meetings and take detailed notes, though they never speak unless asked a direct question by the chair; in some states all public servants are banned from the cabinet room unless required to make a technical presentation on some matter.

Whereas the political domain draws primarily on parliamentarians, their political advisers, the party political machines and the organised lobbies, the policy domain inevitably draws on the wider public sector. Much of the substantive policy development takes place in government agencies, at interdepartmental committees, and on consultative bodies. It relies on expert and impartial bureaucratic advisers. Policy might be finalised in the political forum of cabinet, but this is done frequently on the basis of advice from professional public servants.

This policy world is a rule-bound place, in which submissions and decisions follow strict formats, with clear roles ascribed to central agencies, keen to maintain the quality and accuracy of cabinet material. The authoritative nature of cabinet decisions demands that choices be reached on the basis of full and relevant information, succinctly stated options, and clear articulation of the advantages and problems of any proposal.

## Government as administration

To be effective, policies rely on the resources and power of government. Once choices are made, activity must be directed to achieving the intended objective. This is the domain of administration, in which services are delivered, taxes collected and laws enforced.

In this domain resides the public service, that collection of departments and agencies, staff and resources making up the machinery of government. Here ministers preside, with responsibility to the parliament for the administrative detail of how staff, money and other resources are deployed, how policies are implemented, and whether they realise the objectives set by government. However, it is departmental chiefs and senior executives who do much of the day to day policy work.

Indeed, the division of labour between minister and public servant becomes crucial in the administrative domain. Ministers rely on chief executives to understand and pursue their political priorities, and on public servants to act in the interests of the government of the day. Ministers have little time or capacity for close involvement in the work of their portfolio: their interest is captured by endless consultation with interest groups, electoral matters, parliament and media activities. Ministerial staff often keep a watching brief, and may be a source of friction as they seek to intervene in departmental matters, to drive administrative activity in the direction required by the government. Most policy implementation, though, takes place deep within the public service, far from political eyes. Ministers must find ways to assert control while allowing the professional public service to get on with its tasks.

Three instruments assist cabinet to maintain some authority over the public service — the architecture of government, an annual budget and rules setting out personnel policies.

Traditionally, the *design of government* is the responsibility of the prime minister, chief minister or premier. Departments can be created or abolished through administrative order, though changes to a statutory body usually require consideration by parliament. Incoming leaders often rearrange departmental titles and responsibilities to reflect their own priorities; a Canadian study has tracked in detail how successive prime ministers in Ottawa restructured central agencies to match their 'personal philosophies of leadership, management styles, and political objectives' (Aucoin, 1986:90).

Reorganisation allows leaders to provide a sense of direction and purpose for their governments. In 1987 Bob Hawke restructured the entire federal bureaucracy around a 'micro-economic reform' agenda. Nearly a decade later, incoming prime minister John Howard signalled a shift in federal policy by downgrading some functions inherited from Labor, while providing extra positions and offices for those policy concerns of particular interest to the coalition. State premiers

> I don't think ministers are as powerful as outside opinion would have them appear to be. The terrible thing that isn't acknowledged in Australia is that things are expected of government that government can't deliver.
>
> A federal minister, quoted in Pat Weller and Michelle Gratton, 1981:180

such as Jeff Kennett have imposed radically different structures on their government.

If the architecture of government symbolises the grand design, an *annual budget* is an opportunity for ministers to get into the detail of departmental operations. The 1980s saw significant improvements in financial control technology, as computers, new accounting systems and program structures allowed central agencies, especially treasury and finance departments, to track financial performance with improved precision (Wanna et al., 1992:92ff). Such data in turn allows greater political scrutiny of public sector activity.

Budget processes are, in effect, an annual review and statement of policy in every area of government operation. Commonwealth and state governments rely on an Expenditure Review Committee (ERC), or its equivalent, to work through portfolio plans. The ERC is chaired by the prime minister or treasurer, but includes senior ministers and is assisted by officials from central agencies. It first sets broad financial parameters for the year ahead and then makes allocations across portfolios and programs. Ministers appear before the committee to argue a case. Optimists seek an additional allocation for new programs; realists hope to leave with their budget intact or cut by no more than the average. Across the board reductions in administrative expenditure, usually termed 'efficiency dividends', have become a standard part of the budget process.

*Rules* governing public service employment and operations are less dramatic than budget cycles, but can also be important in shaping agency activity. Public services across the nation are governed by legislation that typically describes a permanent, merit-selected, equitable, impartial public sector outside the direct control of ministers. Some of these attributes no longer pertain in practice. Permanence has little effective meaning, since large-scale redundancies are now a common feature of public service life. Indeed, the principle of tenure is no longer available to senior officers, who must sign five-year contracts and are subject to removal at any time by the government.

The issue of merit selection has been even more contentious. The ideal of a non-partisan public service clashes with the desire of many ministers for political appointments to senior positions. The emerging resolution has seen limited term political appointments, particularly in central agencies.

> When things haven't gone well for you, call in a secretary or a staff man and chew him out. You will sleep better and they will appreciate the attention.
> Lyndon Johnson

Prime Minister John Howard, for example, has established a Cabinet Policy Unit within his department, with a small number of staff appointed on the same terms as those in ministerial offices. On coming to office, John Howard also removed six departmental secretaries. Some states have amended public sector legislation to allow a number of partisan appointments within the senior executive service, and all pay particular attention to the selection of chief executive officers. Australia has not entirely embraced the American 'spoils' system, where each new administration replaces the entire senior ranks of government with its own supporters, but the line between politics and the public sector is blurring in some jurisdictions.

## Bringing the players together

Government requires coordination across each of the political, policy and administrative domains. Some players cross more than one domain, and all look to the centre for coherence. Each domain is represented at the centre of government through figures who can speak with authority for their area of responsibility. In Canberra, the political world is represented by ministers and by the prime minister's chief of staff. The policy domain speaks through the Cabinet Policy Unit and the heads of central agencies

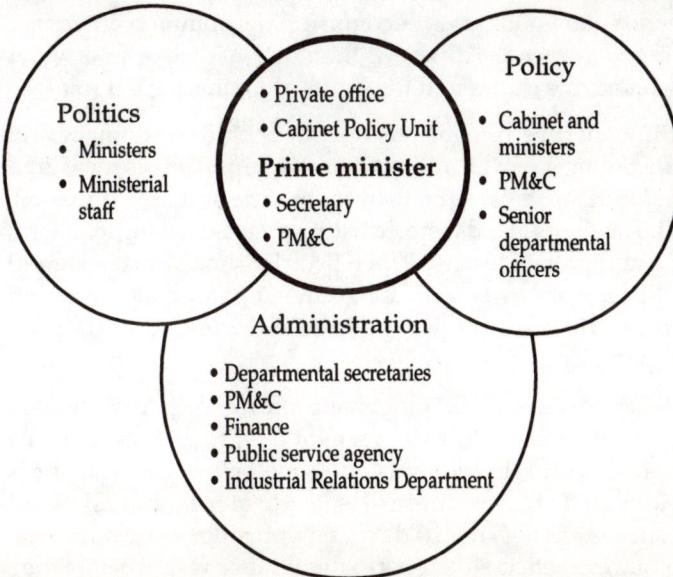

**Figure 2.1** Coordinating the three spheres of government.
(Source: based on Davis, 1996:28)

The Institutions of Public Policy        17

such as PM&C, Finance and Treasury, though policy itself is typically developed within the relevant policy department. The central agencies also speak for the final domain, administration. Similar configurations are found in most states. Figure 2.1 sketches the centre of Commonwealth government, the core executive, to show how the domains cluster around the prime minister.

A key leadership task is to bring the three domains into alignment, so all aspects of government work in concert toward shared goals. An effective prime minister uses proximity to each of the domains as a basis for coordinating government. From the leader's point of view, the intersection of political, policy and administrative domains organises information and advice around a small group at the centre of government. With just a few people in the room, the prime minister can discuss strategic issues from different angles, and judge how a particular proposal might sit within the government's overall program.

Those who work in each domain understand they must play a specific role. If politicians or ministerial advisers, they worry about politics and the media. Policy staff focus on cabinet procedures and documents. Administrators ensure programs are implemented, run effectively and evaluated. Making the system work often requires dividing tasks into manageable pieces. Further, politicians and officers often talk across the boundaries, recognising the common enterprise of government. All know, though, their place in a wider scheme, the duties and the limits of their assigned roles.

Different time dimensions operate within the domains. In the political world, all issues are urgent. Time is measured in hours or days, as controversies flare and are addressed. The media demands immediate responses, making long term planning a rare luxury. When British Prime Minister Harold Wilson said 'a week is a long time in politics' he conveyed the rapid turnover in people and ideas marking his experience.

Policy advisers, on the other hand, are locked into the weekly cycle of cabinet. They operate in a more orderly and rule bound world, in which every issue before government is subjected to a standardised form of analysis and consideration. The '10 day rule' for cabinet consideration requires agencies to prepare submissions weeks before they are brought to cabinet, allowing time for consultation and modification. While occasional urgent items disrupt the

---

> The ubiquity of routines often makes political institutions appear to be bureaucratic, rigid, insensitive or stupid. The simplification provided by rules is clearly imperfect, and the imperfection is often manifest, especially after the fact. But some of the major capabilities of modern institutions come from their effectiveness in substituting rule-bound behaviour for individually autonomous behaviour. Routines make it possible to coordinate many simultaneous activities in a way that makes them mutually consistent. Routines help avoid conflicts; they provide codes of meaning that facilitate interpretation of ambiguous worlds; they constrain bargaining within comprehensible terms and enforce agreements ...
>
> James March and Johan Olsen, 1989:24

routines of decision making, the policy domain is less subject to the roar and tumult of political life.

Administration, too, follows a pattern, often using an annual cycle of budgets, strategic plans, program evaluations and staff appraisal. Accountability and management requirements are served through a predictable, repetitive sequence of tasks. For those busy delivering services, the political world can seem remote and even irrelevant.

These different temporal cycles encourage each domain to develop its own characteristic routines and language. Political advisers speak in ways that may seem brutal and blunt to a policy adviser or program manager, yet they express no more than the imperatives of their world, and the inevitably short time frame available to solve pressing problems. Public servants, in turn, can seem too concerned with process and propriety for ministers and their advisers. The task of those at the centre is to ensure communication remains open, so the domains can function together.

## Coordination through routines

To achieve coherence across the domains of politics, policy and administration, governments rely on routines — those standardised procedures that structure decision making. Cabinet processes are the most visible routine. They organise information, pass proposals through a single channel for consideration, and record decisions made by government. Each domain has its own set of routines — standard operating procedures that remind players who can make decisions, what information is required, and what steps must be taken in particular circumstances. Routines are the standard repertoire of any institution, those 'rules and codes which guide action and give effect to values' (Davis, 1995:25).

The policy cycle presented in this *Australian Policy Handbook* is a routine for decision making. Each step carries its own sequence of procedures and processes, rules and conventions. The overall routine aims to gather information about a problem, assemble evidence and opinion, secure a decision, implement a course of action, and then begin the cycle again through evaluation and rethinking. Yet it does more than just structure actions within government. Routines legitimise power. If cabinet alone can make a particular decision, and if cabinet will only consider a submission prepared according to particular rules, then all players along the way understand their tasks and the lines

> A *routine* is a rule used in making decisions that has the following traits: it is employed widely among people who make certain types of decisions; it focuses their attention on a limited number of the considerations that are potentially relevant to their decision, and thereby simplifies decisions that might have been complex; at the same time, it excludes certain considerations from the decisions, and contributes to political stability by making the decisions predictable under most conditions.
> 
> Ira Sharkansky, 1970:3

of authority established by the routine. In this way routines guide action, but also tell us who is authorised to make a choice, and how that choice will be reached. The routines required for a policy cycle are the essential mechanisms of government, and a continual reminder of who governs within the Australian political system.

The map of government we provide in this chapter complements the more traditional responsible government model. From both perspectives, 'ministers are on top, public servants on tap'. Yet seeing government as three interacting tasks, a meeting of political, policy and administrative routines, provides a sense of the close working relationships found at the centre of government. This model reinforces the notion that effective policy making requires people not only to understand their roles, but to learn to accommodate the differing needs of other players. As Sir Paul Hasluck (1968:1), a former Australian foreign minister and later governor-general, once noted, 'the public service cannot avoid politics any more than fish can avoid the water in which they swim'. Likewise, ministers cannot avoid the public service. Both maximise their influence by learning from, and accommodating, the other.

# Chapter 3
# A Policy Cycle

If our system of government is to produce viable public policies, some order must arise from the endless interaction of political, policy and administrative worlds. That order is achieved through systems that define the roles of each player and their respective responsibilities and channel policy ideas along a recognised sequence on their way to cabinet consideration.

This chapter describes how a policy cycle can be used to understand and structure policy development. The most influential ways of describing policy making are those that break the policy process into clear and identifiable steps. As early as 1951, Harold Lasswell was characterising policy making as a sequence of intelligence, recommendation, prescription, invocation, application, appraisal and termination. Later writers stayed with the idea of steps, but offered variations on the labels, usually suggesting that policy making is a sequence of problem identification, agenda setting, adoption, implementation and policy evaluation (Sabatier and Jenkins-Smith, 1993:2).

For example, Anderson (1994:37) suggests that choices follow a 'commonsense' sequence —

- getting the government to consider action on the problem
- what is proposed to be done about the problem
- getting the government to accept a particular solution to the problem
- applying the government's policy to the problem
- asking 'did the policy work'?

This *Australian Policy Handbook* works within that tradition by adopting a policy cycle approach. It suggests policy develops through a standard sequence of tasks that can be framed as activities or questions. The policy cycle presented

> **Snapshot**
> A policy cycle brings a system and a rhythm to a world that might otherwise appear chaotic and unordered.
>
> This chapter describes a policy cycle that starts with identifying issues, then moves through analysis and implementation to evaluation of the policy's effects. The cycle is a tool, a guide designed to inject rigour but not to limit potential and creativity.

here has been developed because it is a useful organising device, with a range of strengths —

- the policy cycle approach stresses that government is a *process*, and not just a collection of venerable institutions. A cycle conveys movement of ideas and resources, the iteration of policy making, and a process that does not finish with a decision but carries through to implementation and evaluation
- it *disaggregates* complex phenomena into manageable steps, allowing us to focus on the different issues and needs of each phase in the cycle
- a policy cycle allows some *synthesis* of existing knowledge about public policy. We incorporate appropriate literature at the relevant step in the cycle, so locking key lessons from policy making studies into the overall sequence
- it serves as a *description* of policy making, to assist in making sense of policy development, past and present
- it is *normative*, suggesting a particular sequence as an appropriate way to approach the policy task.

The normative values in a policy cycle are deliberate and explicit. Policy making is not a strictly logical pursuit, but a complex and fascinating matrix of politics, policy and administration. When electoral considerations, budget constraints and implementation problems pull in different directions, problems might be open to multiple solutions, or no solution at all. No single procedure guarantees a successful result; governments can make howling errors even using the most rigorous and exact policy processes.

## Alternatives to the policy cycle

Many other models have been developed to bring order to the political-policy-administrative maelstrom. Some of note include Burch and Wood's (1989) analogy that portrays government as a firm, taking public and private resources on the supply side of the manufacturing process, producing goods and services, rules and regulations and transfer payments as policy outputs. Feedback to government through the citizenry influences future supply side choices. This model is illustrated in Figure 3.1.

Richard Simeon (1976:556) describes a 'funnel of causality' that allows policy to be understood at different levels. At

> ... it is *logically* impossible to understand any reasonably complicated situation — including almost any policy process — without some theoretical lens ('theory', 'paradigm', or 'conceptual framework') distinguishing between the set of potentially important variables and causal relationships and those that can safely be ignored.
>
> Paul Sabatier and Hank Jenkins-Smith, 1993:xi

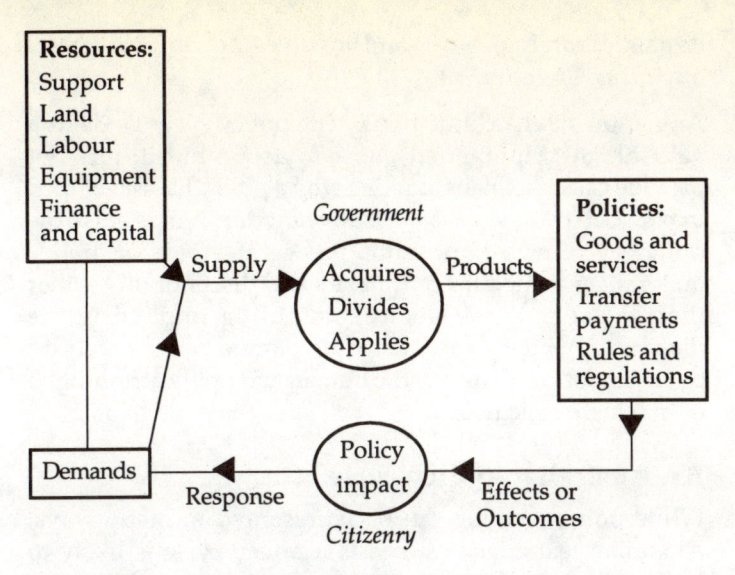

**Figure 3.1** A 'policy process' approach
(Source: from Burch and Wood, 1989:15).

the funnel's widest point, policies are responses to social and economic settings, attempting to steer people and institutions towards goals. The narrower the funnel, the more immediate the factors that come into play, until at its narrowest, we see only those matters relevant to the policy under examination. Simeon's model is a powerful reminder that policy is context dependent, and reflects the dominant thinking of the day. (Consider, for example, discredited restrictive immigration policies of the past. It is easy to detect the cultural values that guided the policy. But which contemporary policies, apparently now so natural and logical, will in the future prove to be just as obviously a product of their times?)

Other models focus on the many participants in the policy process. Sabatier and Jenkins-Smith (1993) offer an 'advocacy coalition framework' that describes policy making in areas subject to long-term negotiation between government and interest groups. They argue that the interaction between coalition of interests, policy brokers and political institutions produces a policy community that discusses ideas and develops a shared understanding of the problem, even while disagreeing about the solution. Environmental policy is one area ripe for analysis using this model, given the strong interactions between 'green' groups and industry as they work with government through consultative committees. This model reminds us that policy making is an ongoing

> The important point about the policy cycle approach is that it usefully suggests that the policy process can be broken down into elements. But there are problems with the approach ... The emphasis upon phases suggests some kind of chronological sequence which is inevitably involved in policy making. We believe the process to be more fluid ...
>
> Martin Burch and Bruce Wood, 1989:16

dynamic, rarely one-off, and involves powerful interests other than government.

Any approach has limitations. The policy cycle model is a valuable description and guide to action but it does not provide causal explanations for why a policy has developed in particular ways. As a normative model there is a risk the policy cycle may impose too great a neatness on policy making, renowned for complexity and discontinuity rather than the relentlessly logical unfolding implied in the diagram. A policy cycle helps us pursue better practices, but it cannot tame entirely the human and political imbroglio of making public policy.

## An Australian policy cycle

While policy making can be represented in many ways, Australian experience suggests a policy cycle is likely to begin with issue identification, and then proceed through policy analysis, policy instruments, consultation, coordination, decision, implementation and evaluation.

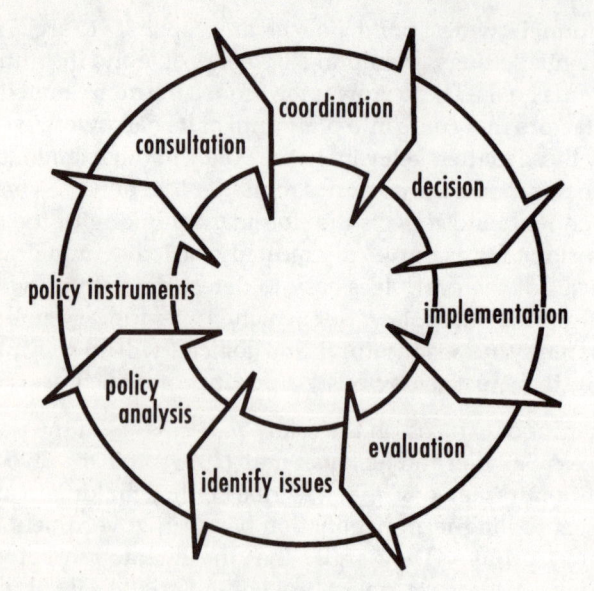

**Figure 3.2** The Australian policy cycle

Much policy begins with *identifying issues*. A new problem emerges in private discussions with interest groups, or in the media, with demands for government action. Sometimes an existing policy proves no longer effective and requires an overhaul — there is never a shortage of people telling government what it should be doing. Issues have many sponsors, and proponents compete to attract attention for their cause. Indeed, much of politics is about defining an agenda for public policy.

Once an issue has caught the eye of government, *policy analysis* becomes important, for without information it will be difficult to frame options. With long standing problems, governments may be guided by their overall party philosophy and program. New issues, though, demand research and reflection. Policy analysis is often, though not always, the work of the public service, drawing on broader debates among specialists in a policy field. It is designed to provide decision makers with sufficient information about the policy problem to make an informed judgement, and typically takes the form of briefing papers for senior officials and ministers.

Should government intervention appear likely, policy analysis leads to identification of appropriate *policy instruments*. Some problems require legislation, others adjustment to the internal operations of government agencies. It is not sufficient to understand a problem, since little will be achieved if the likely policy response is not targeted and plausible; analysis must carry through to recommending policy responses.

One important method to test the strength of the analysis, and the feasibility of the proposed response, is *consultation*. The architecture of government tends to duplication and overlap, since many problems draw in a wide range of players. Early intervention programs for children with intellectual disabilities, for example, can be the responsibility of welfare, health or education departments. All these agencies have something to contribute to policy solutions, and each will be vitally interested in any proposed policy changes. Within government, therefore, it is essential to discuss proposed policy initiatives with related agencies. Policy consultation will probably include discussions with non-government interests (such as clients and families in our example). In many complex areas, government relies heavily on the expertise of those working in the field (such as early intervention professionals). Through consultation, policy proposals are improved, ideas tested and, when appropriate, support gathered.

Once a policy proposal is ready for consideration by the government, issues of *coordination* arise. This typically requires discussions with treasury about available funding

> In a sense everything in the policy world is really just process, the movement of people and programs around common problems such as education, transport and employment. None of the initiatives in these fields stays fixed for very long because the problems themselves keep moving and changing. We cannot afford, therefore, to view policy as just a study of decisions or programs. The specific decisions which often interest us are merely important punctuation marks within this flow — not the thing itself.
>
> Mark Considine, 1994:3–4

for a policy, and with other central agencies over the relation between a new proposal and overall government direction. Coordination may also be necessary to resolve issues between agencies sharing an interest in a field; mechanisms such as interdepartmental committees bring together related agencies and work toward agreement on a common policy strategy.

As the cycle proceeds, a policy issue is identified, analysed, matched with appropriate instruments, discussed with relevant interests, and tested against central policy and financial considerations. The time for a *decision* has arrived. In the Australian setting, this means consideration by cabinet. Each week cabinet receives a range of submissions, and must make binding choices about each. If insufficient information is provided, cabinet may require the whole process of identification and analysis to begin again; too much information and cabinet may be unable to work through the detail and achieve a resolution. The art of good policy advice is to provide sufficient information in succinct form and in a format that carries the reader through a logical sequence of steps toward options or a recommendation. Good policy advice also recognises that the final judgement properly belongs with ministers and not public servants.

The cycle does not conclude with a cabinet decision. *Implementation* must follow, in which the policy is given expression through legislation or a program, in pursuit of the goals agreed by ministers.

And since policies in practice often drift from the objectives of the original submission or are imperfect in realising their goals, *evaluation* is essential so government can gauge the effects of a policy and adjust or rethink policy design as appropriate. Such evaluation, of course, starts the cycle afresh, with a new look at the problem, and a reconsideration of the recommended instruments. Policy is a wheel continually turning, a task never completed.

## The policy cycle and institutions

Much of the work implied in the policy cycle is undertaken by public servants. However, the cycle ranges across all the institutions of the Australian political system. Cabinet submissions have political, policy and administrative implications, and each of these domains will be involved throughout the cycle. Input varies, depending on the political prominence of the issue.

> A good policy process is the vital underpinning of good policy development. Of course, good process does not necessarily guarantee a good policy outcome, but the risks of bad process leading to a bad outcome are very much higher.
>
> Michael Keating, 1996:63

Consider, for example, how the Commonwealth government might respond to changing patterns of aircraft usage of Sydney Airport discussed in Table 3.1.

In this example, policy proceeds in linear fashion through the policy cycle. Because of political pressure, a 'whole of government' approach emerges quickly. There is, however, a tendency for 'parallel processing' within government. Even if the politicians had not picked up the first signs of community and industry distress, routine bureaucratic processes would have collected and analysed airport usage data and advised the minister. Ideas and problems do not come from just one source, but are traded across government. Some policy proposals emerge from political considerations, others are more administrative in character. All will journey through the policy cycle but the trajectory of each will be unique.

## Good process and good policy

A policy cycle is a first foray into complexity. It organises observations into familiar patterns, and provides a guide for future action. It suggests a process that transcends particular institutions or policy designs, a process that can carry decision makers through a simple sequence. Yet the claims made for a policy cycle (or any other model of policy making) must be modest. In political life processes tend to be shaped by problems, with each issue facing government demanding attention in its own way. The dilemmas of making policy do not resemble a 'Gordian knot awaiting the cut of a single superior technique'. Policy is a 'discontinuous series of actions, played out simultaneously across multiple arenas, given unity only through the selection and synthesis of a narrator' (Davis and Weller, 1987:384). Used carefully, a policy cycle can go some way to construct a narrative. And like all good stories, it suggests ways we might behave in future, and so shapes the world it describes.

The policy cycle model begs the question: 'does good process lead to good policy?' Experience shows that good process is integral to consistently good policy. While some very poor policies have grown out of the most rigorous process, it is rarer for good policy to grow from a haphazard approach.

Consistently good policy will only be developed by combining rigour of both process and intellect. The best process in the world cannot substitute for high quality thinking and analysis. Likewise, the most creative and

---

Problems are not always clearly defined, values and goals conflict, time and information for analysis is limited and techniques for comparing options are often crude and unreliable. Policies are not required one at a time but are interconnected so that to ameliorate one problem may be to aggravate another. Causal links cannot always be established, so a technically rational option may have disastrous unanticipated consequences ...

This is not the counsel of despair, but a warning against simplistic prescriptions. When problems are intertwined, goals a moveable feast and resources limited, then only approximations are possible. Australian administrators, like their political masters, are pragmatic. If techniques which consistently improved policy were available, they would be used.

Glyn Davis and Patrick Weller, 1987:384

technically exacting thinking can fail to produce good policy if there is no process to integrate the complex web of activities that marks any public policy endeavour.

**Table 3.1** Hypothetical policy development for Sydney air traffic

|  | Political domain | Policy domain | Administrative domain |
|---|---|---|---|
| **Identifying issues** | Community groups and local authorities become politically active about aircraft noise<br><br>Passengers and airlines complain to MPs and ministers about landing and take-off delays<br><br>Party organisations receive grass roots pressure for formal policy adjustments | Department of Transport (DoT) policy staff monitor international trends in aircraft noise and air traffic management on an ongoing basis | Noise and traffic data captured and analysed, with usage and demand patterns monitored<br><br>Developments in aircraft engineering and feasibility of fleet improvements monitored |
| **Policy analysis** | Minister takes issues of noise and congestion to cabinet for information | Interdepartmental Committee (IDC) established to consider options. Membership covers central agencies (PM&C, Finance) and transport, tourism, business, environment and economic development agencies | Briefing paper sent to minister covering issues and possible responses strategies<br><br>Agencies strengthen data gathering and analysis, and contribute to IDC deliberations through scientific and technical advice |
| **Policy instruments** | 'No aircraft noise' lobby presses for new airport located outside Sydney city area<br><br>Transport and business lobbies press for third runway to provide short term relief<br><br>Local authorities and community groups press for rerouting of aircraft and banning of high-noise craft | IDC notes existing policy limits. Works to integrate safety issues, ground transport needs and noise reductions into cohesive set of instruments<br><br>Costs of curfew downtime and economics of fleet replacement examined | Line agencies provide IDC with detailed technical data on traffic volumes, ground transport needs for various alternative airport sites, and noise reduction strategies<br><br>Finance examines cost parameters of additional runways, inner-city transport corridor improvement, second airport sites and associated transport corridor needs |
| **Consultation** | Sydney Airport Community Forum formed, including community, industry, local councils, and state and federal members of parliament<br><br>Community and industry groups coalesce into organised lobbies, prepare detailed submissions and media campaigns<br><br>Ministers called on to meet with lobby groups who express dissatisfaction with lack of progress on decision | Agencies speak with interest groups about policy options and desired outcomes<br><br>Data analysis for policy implications | Line agencies meet with lobby groups to hear concerns. Data gathered from the various interest groups and local authorities |

|  | **Political domain** | **Policy domain** | **Administrative domain** |
|---|---|---|---|
| **Coordination** | Politicians press for a decision by the responsible ministers<br><br>Issue appears on agenda for meeting of Commonwealth and state ministers | DoT consults with PM&C and Finance about options.<br><br>DoT prepares cabinet submission and passes drafts to key agencies through cabinet secretariat<br><br>Concerns of central agencies and other lines agencies noted and commentary provided in revised submission | Line agencies continue monitoring and consultation, feeding data through to ministers and cabinet and the IDC |
| **Decision** | Cabinet considers submission and accepts a package of improvements to existing capacity, long-term construction of a second airport, noise reductions through curfews, aircraft noise emission standards and rerouting of aircraft to spread noise pollution less densely over affected areas. Noise insulation subsidies for affected inner city suburbs and other measures are also to be implemented<br><br>Details of the second airport are to be further explored in a new phase of decision making | PM&C records and circulates the decisions | Agencies receive advice of decision and distribute to relevant staff for implementation action |
| **Implementation** | Minister announces cabinet's decision, distributes media kits, and tours third runway site<br><br>Sydney Airport Community Forum advised of proposed action<br><br>Airlines advised of noise emission standards to be implemented by regulation, new routes to be followed by aircraft and new operating hours | DoT commences work on third airport options (starting a new policy cycle on this issue) | Finance arranges for funding of options<br><br>DoT prepares regulations implementing curfew and noise emission standards<br><br>Eligibility criteria set down for noise insulation subsidy and application process put in place; affected residents advised through media campaign |
| **Evaluation** | Industry and community groups continue to press competing claims<br><br>Media commentary is critical of some aspects of the decision<br><br>Industry continues to lobby against the curfew and complain about delays in airport access<br><br>Community group activity shifts in response to changes with new players emerging | Ministers require regular briefing on progress with implementation and noise and traffic impacts<br><br>IDC continues to meet to consider further developments | Funding needs assessed, and DoT advises Finance and PM&C of expected shortfalls<br><br>Ongoing monitoring of noise and traffic impacts reveal serious problems continue despite third runway and noise reduction measures. |

# Chapter 4
# Identifying Issues

> **Snapshot**
> This chapter looks at how issues are selected for attention from among the myriad of matters pressed on government. Many topics vie for attention but few are chosen.
>
> Policy professionals need to understand how issues arise, and how key concerns may be overlooked if they do not attract political interest.

Political life is contested around issues. Parties and interest groups, parliament and media, departments and private companies all compete to draw attention to their key issues. Politics becomes an argument about which topics have a legitimate right to government responses and public resources.

## The policy agenda

The outcome of this contest is a 'policy agenda'. A policy agenda represents the narrowing of an infinite array of possible policy problems to those few that command government interest. When an issue is identified it becomes part of the policy cycle, subject to analysis, policy instrument development and so on round the circle. There is a crucial moment in the policy cycle, a point at which a private concern is transformed into a policy issue. Suddenly the concern commands the resources of government, while a myriad of others languish as merely private concerns. No wonder competition among issue advocates is so fierce.

This chapter examines how and why topics are accorded this privilege. It explores the ways an issue becomes important enough for government to commit resources, by looking first at the nature of the drivers of the policy agenda, and then at the nature of policy problems. Policy officers must develop sensitivity to the nature of issues, to minimise surprise and anticipate problems. They must also understand how lobbyists work to influence government agendas, and the self-interested nature of many proposals offered as public policy solutions. The battle to elevate issues to the attention of cabinet is, in microcosm, the struggle of interests and ideas that marks all politics.

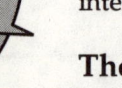

## The agenda metaphor

To speak of a policy 'agenda' is to use a metaphor implying a vast committee with a single set of topics for discussion.

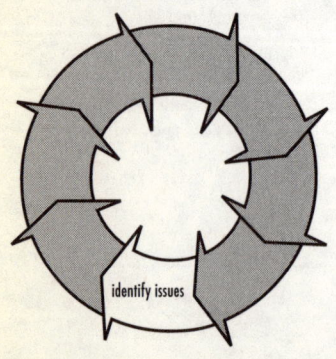

Neither politics nor government is so neat. At any moment there will be urgent issues demanding instant attention, while once pressing problems fade to be almost forgotten. Some issues of narrow but strongly held concern attract no interest at all.

When cabinet meets, ministers do have an agenda, a list of topics for discussion. But this list is only a small sample from the policy agenda, in turn a tiny selection from a universe of possible topics. The idea of a policy agenda is simply a useful reminder that, with limited time and resources, policy makers pay attention to only a few issues and ignore the rest. So what drives some issues on to the agenda and confines others to also-ran status?

## Issue drivers

Much detailed policy advice arises from within government. The domains of politics, policy and administration interact to produce an agenda for government, assign responsibility for preparing options, and draw up a timetable for cabinet consideration and implementation. Yet much that government does is foisted on ministers from outside. Policy cannot ignore the 'issue drivers', those external and internal factors that throw up topics for resolution. Governments have priorities, but rarely can they set the broader policy agenda.

Examples of political issue drivers include —
- party political platforms
- key government achievements of the past
- ministerial and governmental changes.

In theory, ministers are masters of the policy cycle. They decide whether an issue receives attention, and how much. In reality, politicians are subject to an array of external influences — parliament and their colleagues, the party they represent, interest groups and political donors, the media and public opinion. The political agenda reflects a shifting mix of ministerial policy concerns and those external issues that cannot be ignored.

The political domain is volatile, to the point of fragility. The rise or fall of a prominent minister can dramatically shift priorities. When parliaments are finely balanced, as has long been the case with the Senate, an independent member can become a significant source of policy initiatives.

**Politics is not perfect**

Defining a policy agenda through political competition risks some important but unattractive issues missing out — in the same way, endangered but photogenic species such as eagles and bilbies have a better chance of attracting funding and research than less glamorous but also threatened contributors to biodiversity such as sharks and snails.

> A policy agenda is that 'list of subjects or problems to which government officials, and people outside of government closely associated with these officials, are paying some serious attention at any given time'. (John Kingdon, 1995:3)
>
> Kingdon suggests certain circumstances are more likely to gain government attention —
>
> - problems in existing programs are of more interest than new problems
> - politicians are drawn to issues that challenge important values
> - problems attracting unfavourable comparisons with other parts of the country or other nations have more chance of being noticed
> - attaching a problem to an important legal principle may attract renewed interest. For example, providing public transport for people with disabilities became a whole new concern when redefined by interest groups as a civil rights issue.

The ideology of the government party will dictate certain issues. This is clearest immediately after a change in government. For example, the Howard government, elected after 13 years of Labor administration, quickly introduced policy issues different in kind from its predecessor. Industrial relations change became a prominent issue, as did public service reductions. What government decides to pursue will affect what people talk about.

On the other hand, after some years in office the fiery platform of opposition may be exhausted. Governments come to rely more on policy advice and issue identification from within the public sector — despite the growing number of policy 'think tanks', most with decided political views. Still, politics never disappears entirely from the equation. Even long established governments find themselves overtaken by new issues requiring rapid responses.

The political process includes periodic changes within government as a prime minister reshuffles cabinet, and ministers resign or fall from grace. Each change of minister brings the potential for a fresh policy agenda, and for new internal and external influences. Policy professionals learn that an individual minister's preferences are important and must be accommodated within the policy cycle. They also observe that politicians often cannot set the agenda; responding to problems and complaints consumes much ministerial time.

Ministers cannot control the world that buffets government from outside. There are powerful external forces that shape the agenda and demand immediate attention. These same outside forces also limit the policy responses available to government.

Examples of external drivers include —

- economic forces (e.g. share market fluctuations, interest rate adjustments, employment rates, business fortunes)
- media attention
- opinion polls
- legal shifts (e.g. High Court judgments)
- International relations (refugee arrivals, diplomatic representations over human rights issues, wars between other nations)
- technological development (e.g. the Internet as a vehicle for movement of currency outside the existing tax net)

- demographic shifts (e.g. population growth will change patterns of demand for government services).

A sudden dip in the New York stock market can have ripple effects on Australian economic policy. A High Court decision might force a reinterpretation of some policy fundamentals. An influential company or community group can exert great pressure for its private interests to be brought into public policy. A war on another continent shifts resources from one policy activity to another. Drought, flood, fire and cyclone demand attention and money for displaced residents and financially stricken farms and businesses. A lone gunman can change a nation's approach to weapons policy.

Market forces are probably the most powerful precisely because they are beyond the regulation of governments. One might control the rate of, say, industrial relations change, but no government can control the price an Australian commodity fetches in the international market, with its implications for income and employment. Naturally, governments attempt to manipulate such matters (for example, with excises or orderly marketing schemes) but they cannot influence another nation's bumper crop.

There are also factors within government which contribute to the cabinet agenda —

- emerging issues monitored by government policy specialists, who structure information and so shape the political domain's view of the matter
- monitoring policy issues in other jurisdictions (e.g. overseas responses to particular problems, successes or failures of policies in other states)
- ongoing monitoring of 'wicked problems', intractable issues perennially of government concern
- coordination of policy issues across government and between government structures and agendas
- regular, programmed reviews, built into the budget cycle
- statutory 'sunset' dates
- budget overruns
- unfavourable audit reports
- performance audits, and benchmark failures.

Policy professionals must develop sensitivity to these external factors, to prevent surprises that force a government into unplanned costs or worse. A depth of understanding of external policy drivers is a prerequisite to high quality service

> **Examples of external drivers — the law**
>
> The celebrated native title case, *Mabo v Queensland*, restated traditional legal understanding of land titles, and the nature of European occupation of Australian soil. The High Court drew on long-standing legal principles, yet governments took 18 months to agree on a *Native Title Act*.
>
> Contrast the response to the 1993 excise case *Capital Duplicators*. This decision had the potential to remove state power to levy taxes, and result in legal claims for refunds of alcohol, petrol and tobacco taxes collected over past years. Even before the court decided, committees of Commonwealth and state officials developed possible policy responses. Legislation was passed in many jurisdictions in anticipation of a negative outcome for the states. This effort did not bear fruit until 1997 when the High Court did finally strike down the state business franchise taxes.
>
> Powerful external forces each summonsed a policy agenda, yet the capacity and readiness of the various domains to respond was vastly different in the two instances.

> ... politics is about collections of ill-informed opinions moving in one particular direction.
> Alistair McAlpine

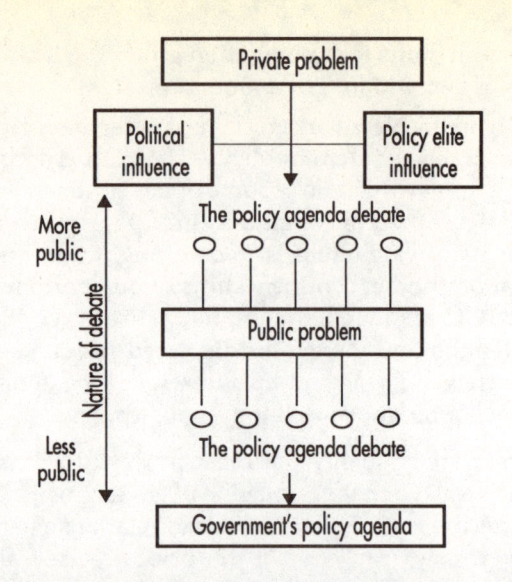

**Figure 4.1** The agenda-setting process

delivery, since that is the basis of an appropriate and rapid response to emerging issues.

While political and external drivers shape much that governments do, policy professionals can also influence the policy agenda. After all, they craft the words considered by cabinet, develop policy models and policy options and control the inner workings of the policy dynamic. Such professionals work in a political context, but their role is not political. Rather, they must provide independent policy advice on the issues of the day — and on those issues which deserve attention but are being ignored.

The responsible government model assumes a permanent, independent public service, bringing continuity and stability to the administration of government. The policy specialist dwells in a grey world that is neither politics nor public administration, but is public policy — that intersection of the political, policy and administrative domains.

## What issues make the agenda?

Cobb and Elder (1972:161–62) suggest that issues have most prospect of attracting the attention of politicians when the topic has mass appeal. An unsaleable issue should be redefined 'as ambiguously as possible, with implications for as many people as possible, involving issues other than the dispute in question ... and as simply as is feasible'.

> An issue arises when a public with a problem seeks or demands governmental action, and there is public disagreement over the best solution to the problem.
> Robert Eyestone, 1978:3

Identifying Issues

There are common steps in how problems develop according to Cobb and Elder. Interest groups, officials and politicians identify a private problem, and strive to make it of concern to the public. If they succeed, the issue becomes part of the policy agenda, with discussion in the media, the legislature and the political process. If government feels it must respond, the issue is assigned to a public institution and so is drawn into the policy cycle. Figure 4.1 illustrates the journey from private problem to bureaucratic concern.

These common steps suggest a typical policy agenda will have several key characteristics. The agenda arises from competition among voices seeking attention. It is determined politically, with no guarantee the most significant issues will break through the pack. The policy agenda is biased toward areas already receiving government attention or with capacity to attract political interest. The agenda is set often not by policy opinion or media attention but by influential elites either already in government or with access to decision makers.

Those who work in the policy process must recognise the potential for important issues to be lost in the crush. The policy agenda is whatever preoccupies government at a particular moment, but this may not be the most important set of problems around. If policy makers rely solely on a mixture of political process, bureaucratic convenience and media enthusiasm to compile an agenda, they will be reacting to a very limited set of interests. Most issues emerge through these familiar processes, but the government agenda can be expanded through regular scanning of economic and social conditions, extensive use of data and indicators, evaluations of policy effectiveness and a willingness to look beyond the easy subjects.

## Issue attention cycle

Whatever the good intentions, government is susceptible to the media, with its capacity to present some issues as 'problems', even 'crises', demanding urgent government attention (Ward 1995). Such topics travel through what Anthony Downs (1972) once labelled an 'issue attention cycle'. Pressure groups try to attract attention for some serious problem, but often must wait until a dramatic event and media coverage carries it on to the policy agenda. Then alarmed discovery and brave promises inspire a scramble by political, policy and administrative players for solutions, followed by growing realisation of the real costs of achieving

> ...each problem must compete for official attention because of limited time and resources. The demands that policymakers choose or feel compelled to act on at a given time, or at least appear to be acting on, constitute the policy agenda ...
> James Anderson, 1994:89

> Issues arise from group conflict. These issues may eventually command a position on the agenda of governmental decision-makers, who manage group conflict. An important way in which an issue may gain access to a governmental agenda is by expanding in scope, intensity, and visibility. These processes are important determinants of where the conflicts will be resolved and how the issues will ultimately be defined, so groups attempt to control them to promote their own interests.
> Roger Cobb and Charles Elder, 1972:160

> **Just how relevant are policy players?**
>
> John Kingdon (1995:199) distinguishes between visible and hidden participants — the very public politicians, political parties and media who champion particular issues, and more shadowy world of specialist bureaucrats, policy advisers and ministerial staff. The chances of an issue attracting government interest are increased 'if that subject is pushed by participants in the visible cluster, and dampened if it is neglected by those participants'. To make the policy agenda, an issue benefits from recognition by visible players and meaningful commitment from those behind the scenes.
>
> An innovative Victorian study, reported by Denis Muller and Bruce Headey (1996) found a range of players influencing agenda setting in an Australian case, in this case a mix of political, economic and bureaucratic elites. Some issues emerge first in policy debate, but many enter the policy process through private interaction among those who have a direct interest in policy outcomes.

change. By the time institutions and budgets have been established, the public has already lost interest and is chasing the next exciting problem. The issue may be largely forgotten, but at least there are now some programs and resources in place.

Not all issues attract even this cycle of attention. Those subjects lacking dramatic impact, that affect only minorities or do not lend themselves to simple analysis and presentation, are unlikely to find an audience. The policy agenda, always constrained, is further restricted when issues must also have entertainment value.

## Identifying issues

There are a number of stages in problem identification. To make the policy agenda and be taken up by government, an issue must meet at least four simple conditions —

- *agreement on a problem*. A problem only exists when significant interests and individuals agree present circumstances are unacceptable. Most issues presented to government fail to find a sponsor. It usually requires a coalition of voices within and outside government to raise an issue to a problem requiring an authoritative response

- *the prospect of a solution*. Even with agreement on the nature of a problem, policy makers prefer issues that offer plausible solutions. Some intractable problems cannot be avoided, but it is easier to sell a topic to cabinet where resolution seems possible. Few politicians are drawn to issues promising certain failure

- *an appropriate issue*. Though policy makers might agree an issue exists and can be addressed, political considerations come into play. Each dollar spent on an issue is a dollar not available for some other program, and cabinet must be persuaded a problem is of sufficient consequence to warrant time and investment

- *a problem for whom?* The ideological framework of the governing party or parties may influence whether ministers wish to deal with an issue at all.

Many problems do not get started in the policy cycle, but die at the issue identification stage. Kingdon (1995:201) uses a provocative biological metaphor: issue identification is like natural selection, in which external factors such as agreement on a problem, or technical feasibility, select out only a few issues for the next stage of the policy cycle. Kingdon stresses just how many problems, issues and ideas fall by the wayside early. Issues judged unacceptable — those 'that do not square with policy community values, that would cost more than the budget will allow, that run afoul of opposition in either the mass or specialised publics, or that would not find a receptive audience among elected politicians — are less likely to survive than proposals that meet these standards'. Unseen, but systematic, biases can distort this judgement, a risk made all the greater when assumptions are not articulated.

> **Issue identification skills**
> - systematic monitoring
> - networking
> - intuitive issue monitoring ('political smarts')
> - ongoing consultation with peak bodies
> - media monitoring
> - inter-agency information exchange
> - issue recording

## Defining problems

Before a policy can tackle some pressing issue, the problem must be given shape and boundaries. Herbert Simon (1973) proposes a key distinction between *ill-structured* and *well-structured* problems.

We encounter ill-structured problems all the time: issues such as poverty or discrimination that demand attention but are open to endless interpretations and potential solutions. To become the object of public policy, such problems must be tightly defined so they can be analysed. A well-structured problem is one open to solution. 'Much problem solving effort is directed at structuring problems, and only a fraction of it at solving problems once they are structured,' argues Simon (1973:187).

To address an ill-structured problem, suggests Simon, we should break it into smaller, well-structured issues. By solving each of these, we address the wider, and still ill-structured, issue.

To define a problem is to shape the options for a solution. How we perceive the problem will influence powerfully the range of potential policy solutions. Only some issues make the agenda, and these may be presented in ways that assist particular interests while ignoring others. The injunction for caution in accepting an agenda defined by others applies also to the way issues are structured.

## Wicked problems

To become subject to public policy, a problem must be given structure. This structure in turn comes from acquiring knowledge about the issue, so boundaries can be drawn and

> A decision deferred is a decision made.
> Harold Wilson

smaller component problems extracted from the larger issue. With structure come the first steps toward problem resolution.

Yet, however well-structured the problem, some issues are not open to solution. Historical factors, competing interests or sunk costs can make all sides to a dispute unwilling to compromise. Government may have to balance priorities between interest rates and inflation levels or between encouraging rural exports and preventing further land degradation. Rittel and Webber (1973) label these 'wicked problems', those issues that cannot be settled and will not go away. Much of social and economic policy is about managing (but not solving) wicked problems. They are a reminder that the capacity of government to impose its will on a recalcitrant world is always limited, and no policy can be permanent or final. Much policy making is not about solving policy problems but about managing policy conflicts. Policy makers who seek 'once and for all solutions' to wicked problems condemn themselves to frustration and failure.

## Non-decisions

One way of avoiding wicked problems, and just plain difficult ones, is not to make a decision at all. Government may find it easier not to discuss a matter than to disappoint some supporters.

More fundamentally, though, non-decisions can be an expression of the same biases that keep issues from the agenda. They are an important exercise of power, an assertion that some matters do not warrant attention from government. Bachrach and Baratz (1963:641) believe non-decisions occur 'when the dominant values, the accepted rules of the game, the existing power relations among groups, and the instruments of force, singly or in combination, effectively prevent certain grievances from developing into full-fledged issues which call for decisions'.

In effect, non-decisions happen when government refuses to define a topic as a problem requiring a public policy.

Not everyone will accept that choice. Much of the political process is about promoting issues. Interest groups, policy advisers and politicians all spend time selling issues they believe do not get sufficient attention from government. There are manuals available for lobbying government, and groups for and against the status quo in many policy areas. A non-decision may not be allowed to close the argument.

A famous, but now out of print, American guide, Saul Alinsky's (1971), *Rules for Radicals: A pragmatic primer for the realistic radical*, offered invaluable advice for those outside government seeking to draw attention to an issue and to manipulate policy process. Its suggestions, and implications for issue identification, are outlined in Table 4.1.

**Table 4.1** Gaining attention for an issue

| Rule for radicals | Issues identification implications |
| --- | --- |
| Power is not only what you have, but what the enemy thinks you have | Issues flow from those who are perceived to have influence of some sort in the political process |
| Never go outside the expertise of your people. Feeling secure stiffens the backbone | Policy issues arise where government has limited capacity to respond before issues become important |
| Whenever possible, go outside the expertise of the enemy. Look for ways to increase insecurity, anxiety and uncertainty | |
| Make the enemy live up to its own rules. If the rule is that every letter gets a reply, send 30,000 | Policy issues are flagged by sudden shifts in the need to respond, or sudden shifts in demand for resources |
| Ridicule is humanity's most potent weapon. There's no defence. It's irrational. It's infuriating. It also works as a key pressure point to force the enemy into concessions | Political and bureaucratic discomfort, and adverse publicity are prime indicators of a policy issue in formation |
| Keep the pressure on. Never let up. Keep trying new tactics to keep the opposition off balance. As the enemy masters one approach, hit them with something new | Consistency of discomfort is an indicator of real or perceived influence |
| A good tactic is one your people enjoy. They'll keep doing it without urging and come back to do more. They'll even suggest better ones | |
| Pick a target and freeze it, personalise it, polarise it. Isolate the target from sympathy. Go after people, not institutions. People hurt faster than institutions | Unfortunate, but often accurate advice |

Identifying Issues

## Issue identification skills

The question of how to identify and define problems has long troubled those seeking a rigorous approach to decision making. Though problem definition is essential to the policy cycle, there can be no single, reliable, prescribed way to proceed. Defining the policy agenda is the point at which creativity, chance and politics, rather than analytical method, are most likely to hold sway.

Public problems are not like games or puzzles, with neatly defined rules and ready solutions. They are mental constructs, abstractions from reality shaped by our values, perceptions and interests. Problems are 'not objective entities in their own right, "out there", to be detected as such, but are rather the product of imposing certain frames of reference' on reality (Dery, 1984:4).

The imprecise and subjective nature of public problems requires a commitment to scanning by policy advisers. They must be prepared to look not just at those issues that make the policy agenda, but at pressing needs that do not find advocates.

# Chapter 5
# Policy Analysis

'Policy analysis is an art,' argued Aaron Wildavksy (1987:15). His purpose was to introduce an important paradox about the policy process. Often, he noted, the subject matter of policy analysis is 'public problems that must be solved at least tentatively to be understood'. Looking for a solution may be necessary before we understand the nature of the issue. To structure a problem is to give it shape and meaning through policy analysis. By the time we have tied down the issue we can already see solutions that might follow.

'Policy analysis' implies a rigorous method. There are important and valuable analytic techniques available to public policy practitioners. But judgement must precede application of any analytic device. How important is this problem? How much time and effort should be expended in seeking a solution? What is the appropriate approach? Sometimes the art is deciding how much science is required.

Policy makers develop shortcuts for these judgements. Emerging problems may be addressed by small changes to existing programs, a process known as incrementalism. Decision makers sometimes cast around for solutions from other jurisdictions, appropriating ideas that have worked elsewhere (Schneider and Ingram, 1988). They recognise the significant investment required to analyse a new problem and develop options. Policy makers know perfect rationality is not available in a world of limited attention and contingent politics, and seek to minimise search time.

Yet those in the policy process must have ways to approach new problems and to rethink old ones. There are issues that do not lend themselves to modifying current practice or to stealing other people's solutions. While perfect rationality may not be available, a sequential approach to policy analysis at least ensures definitions, implications, goals and possible outcomes for a policy have been worked through systematically. In solving public problems, art is important, but method helps.

**Snapshot**

Good decision making about complex issues requires analysis. This is a fundamental stage in the policy cycle, since analysis is the basis for developing options and making decisions.

This chapter explores the role of analysis, sets out a practical series of steps for policy analysis, and locates this within the various analytic frameworks used by government.

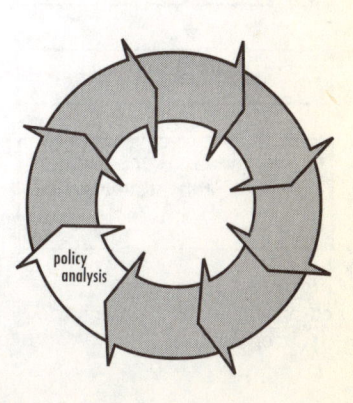

## The purpose of policy analysis

Most government departments have 'policy experts', people who study policy problems and offer solutions. They may comprise a special section of the organisation as a policy unit or each division can assume this role as it develops material for consideration by senior managers. Ministerial offices also take a strong interest in policy analysis, and will seek staff with detailed policy knowledge.

Policy analysis is not decision making. Politicians seek considered advice about issues, a task usually assigned to the bureaucracy, although it may be undertaken by political advisers or external inquiry. Typically the results will be conveyed in a briefing note to a minister or an information paper for cabinet.

Analysis provides data and advice for decision makers. It involves a professional commitment to presenting information in an objective and impartial manner. The purpose of analysis is to help others appreciate the costs and benefits of a range of approaches to a policy problem.

## Rationality

The ideal of a scientific approach to problem solving — logical, value-free, reliable, available for a wide array of problems — is attractive for many. Who would not prefer rational solutions to pressing public problems? How could anyone defend ad hoc, incremental decisions over those reached through careful analysis?

Yet experience suggests rationality is an unusual thing in the complex, quasi-political world of public policy. Rational decision making only occurs when there is agreement on objectives and a clear understanding of means. Such circumstances are rare. They may occur when established policy communities, dealing with familiar problems, develop consensus about an appropriate solution to a problem. Most public policy choices do not rest on such firm foundations, as governments seek to balance contending interests.

Prescriptions for a 'rational' policy process remain influential but unrealised. In its classic form, as illustrated in Figure 5.1, this approach is known as the *'rational comprehensive model* — rational because it follows a logical, ordered sequence, and comprehensive because it canvasses, assesses and compares all options'  (Davis et al., 1993:160–61). While many variations appear in the policy literature, all share six basic

```
┌─────────────────────────────┐
│ Problem identified and      │
│ defined, objective set      │
└──────────────┬──────────────┘
               ▼
┌─────────────────────────────┐
│ Values and goals determined │
│ and ranked in priority order│
└──────────────┬──────────────┘
               ▼
┌─────────────────────────────┐
│    All options identified   │
└──────────────┬──────────────┘
               ▼
┌─────────────────────────────┐
│ Each option tested for costs│
│        and benefits         │
└──────────────┬──────────────┘
               ▼
┌─────────────────────────────┐
│ Cost-benefit ratios compared│
└──────────────┬──────────────┘
               ▼
┌─────────────────────────────┐
│   Decision maker selects    │
│ option that best meets the  │
│         objectives          │
└─────────────────────────────┘
```

**Figure 5.1** The rational comprehensive approach to decision making

and obligatory steps —

1. a problem is identified and defined
2. the values, goals and objectives of those making the decision are made explicit and ranked in priority order
3. all options that could achieve the goal are identified
4. the costs and benefits of each option are made explicit
5. costs and benefits for each option are then compared
6. with information about costs and benefits the decision maker can choose the option that best achieves her or his values, goals and objectives.

> To be rational in any sphere, to display good judgement in it, is to apply those methods which have turned out to work best in it. What is rational in a scientist is therefore often Utopian in a historian or a politician (that is, it systematically fails to obtain the desired result), and vice versa.
> Isaiah Berlin, 1996:30

This model appears regularly in textbooks. So do the criticisms. A rational comprehensive model assumes things about the world that often do not hold — that problems are clear, separate and stable; that decision makers are certain of their values; that goals are hierarchical rather than multiple, conflicting and circumstantial. The model requires consideration of all options, which can be difficult or impossible, and the comparison of options that may not be readily quantifiable.

In practice, decision making is rarely rational (we do not always undertake every step in the model) and hardly ever comprehensive (since political realities, budgets and time usually limit those options worth serious consideration). Yet in setting out a useful sequence for making choices, the model at least forces policy makers to work systematically, and to provide some justification for favoured options. The following sections offer a simplified version of the model, one without the virtues of strict rationality but with the advantages of order and process in addressing policy problems.

## A sequence for policy analysis

There are cycles within the policy cycle. Policy analysts typically work through problems in an orderly way. The analyst's cycle might include —

- formulate the problem
- set out objectives and goals
- identify decision parameters
- search for alternatives
- propose a solution or options.

This sequence does not end the process. Subsequent steps in the policy cycle, such as the selection of instruments, consultation or the political decision making process, may change aspects of the analysis, or even require a fresh evaluation of the problem. Policy analysis is not a 'once and for all' step; as agreement on the nature and scale of the problem varies, so the analysis must shift to take account of new realities.

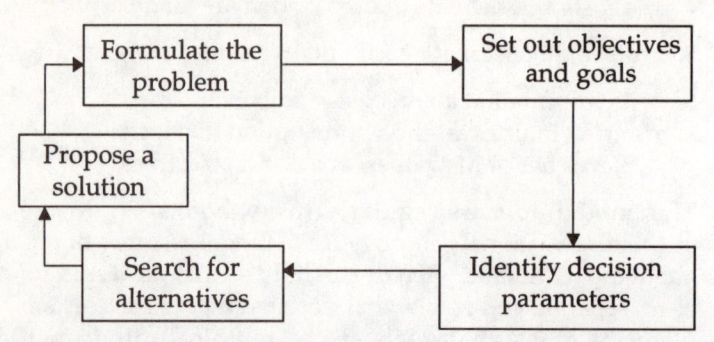

**Figure 5.2** Policy analysis iteration

**Common questions to clarify issues**

How did this situation arise?

Who is affected by this issue and why?

What do the main players in the field say about the issue?

Are there data suggesting trends?

Do local or international studies indicate the probable trajectory of this issue?

Can the problem be broken into smaller parts and dealt with as a series of related issues?

Are there existing programs or processes that can be applied to this problem?

To whom within government does this problem belong?

See, for example, Gary Brewer and Peter deLeon, 1983:43ff.

Policy analysis is invariably iterative, because in practice 'things are seldom tidy' (Quade, 1982:49). Information is often incomplete. People disagree over objectives. Parameters shift. Policy analysts must be reconciled to developing options, testing them against departmental and ministerial opinion, and then working through again and again.

*Formulating the problem*

The first step to policy advice is to *formulate the problem*. Generally only some external process — lobbying by an interest group, media campaigns or a persistent failure of programs to achieve objectives — draws the attention of decision makers to an issue. Ministers then seek advice from the bureaucracy about the nature, scale and characteristics of the concern.

There is no single method for formulating problems because the particular scale and content of the issue, and the way it is originally discussed, tend to frame the research which follows. Each problem may be unique.

Formulating a problem immediately raises questions of ownership. Departments have characteristic ways of seeing the world, and may define issues in ways that complement existing missions. Jeremy Taylor (1995) has explored how health, welfare and education departments in three Australian states respond to the question of early intervention programs for children under five years of age with intellectual disabilities. He demonstrates that each department formulates the 'problem' in a way that draws these children into its own programs and priorities. It requires a major commitment to cross-departmental coordination before target children receive multi-disciplinary treatment that begins with their needs rather than bureaucratic convenience.

Australian governments rely on a number of institutional constraints, including consultation prior to cabinet decisions and evaluation of policy proposals by central agencies, to restrain too narrow or self-interested problem specification. There remains, though, a professional obligation on policy analysts to offer options that can be defended on their own terms, and do not simply reflect personal or departmental values.

## Objectives and goals

Defining objectives is fundamental to making policy choices. The objectives selected will 'determine what priorities are assigned and what policies are selected, provide guidelines for the implementation of the chosen programs, and determine the criteria for program evaluation' (Brewer and deLeon, 1983:48).

Just as problem definition can be a moving feast, so tying decision makers to particular objectives may prove difficult. Problems tend to pose precise questions ('How much will we spend to address this concern?') while politicians prefer to keep answers general ('Let's look at it in an overall budget context'). Government policy documents set out principles but often do not provide sufficient information to inform policy development in a specialised field.

Further, all policy decisions are taken in a wider setting. Since an ideal health care system would consume much of the national product, health system solutions are compromises. The goal remains unchanged — quality of care — but in practice this objective is balanced against other, non-health, considerations.

As Wildasvksy (1987:216) observes, 'the objectives people have, the goals they seek to achieve, are a function not merely of their desirability but also of their feasibility. What we try to do depends to some degree on what we can do.'

> Objectives are not just out there, like ripe fruit waiting to be plucked; they are manmade, artificial, imposed on a recalcitrant world. Inevitably they do violence to reality by emphasising some activities (hence organisational elements) over others. Thus the very step of defining objectives may be considered a hostile act. If they are too vague, no evaluation can be done. If they are too specific, they never encompass all the indefinable qualities that their adherents insist they have. If they are too broad, any activity may be said to contribute to them. If they are too narrow, they may favour one segment of the organisation over another. Strategically located participants often refuse to accept definitions of objectives that would put them at a disadvantage or in a straight-jacket should they wish to change their designation of what they do in the future. Arguments about which really, but really and truly, are the objectives of the organisation may stultify all future action.
> 
> Aaron Wildavksy, 1987:216

To deal with ambiguous or conflicting objectives, policy analysts typically produce a range of options for decision makers. Each option presents a different configuration of problem definition, policy objective and proposed solution. Ministers can then choose among an array of values and opportunities. As with problem definition, shaping options imposes an ethical requirement on analysts to treat the alternatives fairly.

*Identify decision parameters*

Policy advisers can frame options once they know —

- the likely objectives of the minister and government
- the possibilities for obtaining additional resources
- the time frames required for consideration and action
- the relative priority of the problem.

Often departments prepare briefing notes to test the minister's concern and resolve on an issue. If the minister indicates interest, further options or a single policy proposal are then prepared.

If the minister does not take up the invitation, the department must either find ways of rearranging its own priorities, or leave the problem unaddressed. Every new problem is pushing on to the agenda of government, already crowded with more demands than ministers can satisfy. The iterative process of notes and briefings between the department and the minister's office provides an indication for policy analysts about the relative importance of some new issue.

As constraints on any policy program become clear, analysts can judge how much time and attention a problem deserves. If the issue is unlikely to attract strong interest, policy makers may lean to an incremental solution — a minor modification of an existing program, or an extension of familiar procedures to a new domain. This minimises search and analysis time.

On other hand, policy makers may confront new problems for which incremental solutions are not available. Analysis is required to create new laws, programs or institutions. Much greater investment must occur in research and evaluation before a policy approach emerges (Hayes 1992).

Sometimes, even with that investment, viable policy options are not available. This may reflect a lack of reliable information about the problem at hand, leading to —

- inability to break the problem into separate, manageable units
- lack of confidence in the causal models informing policy options
- incapacity to cost various courses of action.

When analysis fails, and the parameters affecting a decision remain unclear, this is usually a warning. It suggests policy makers are dealing with a 'wicked problem' likely to defy policy intervention.

It would be wrong just to ignore such problems, but policy advisers must be honest in their appraisal. A minister needs to know if a problem has no solution. President Johnson accepted advice from his cabinet and staff that the war in Vietnam could be won. In retrospect, he lacked accurate information about the problem. The White House did not have a reliable causal model about the likely course of events, or a realistic assessment of the cost of victory. Had the president's advisers been more honest about their limited knowledge of the region and its history, and provided a wider range of options, Johnson may not have elected to destroy his presidency pursuing a tragic, deadly and doomed policy.

Of course, honest appraisal may include revisiting issue identification, because sometimes failure to develop viable options reflects muddy thinking about the nature of the problem itself. Indeed, revisiting issue identification is probably a necessary reality test even when viable options are developed.

### Search for alternatives

The *search* phase of analysis requires research. The objective is to acquire as much relevant information as required, and to identify possible responses. Given that problems often have multiple faces (economic, social, environmental, legal, technical, political), a team approach to analysis can be important.

Sources for ideas may include —

- current policies locally and in other jurisdictions
- international findings on best practice in the field
- recent reviews and reports on the issue
- academic journals

> **Good policy advice**
>
> Michael Keating (1996:62), former Secretary of the Department of Prime Minister and Cabinet, suggests four key elements to good policy advice —
>
> - is the advice timely, forward looking, correctly recognising emerging issues and problems
> - does it identify implications of options, alternatives and cost effective solutions
> - does it form part of a clearly defined and coherent strategy, including a strategy for achieving acceptance of the policy, and
> - is it practical to implement?

> **Analytic frameworks and examples**
>
> **Economic framework**
> - cost-benefit
> - cost-effectiveness
> - opportunity costs
> - market competitiveness
> - regulatory impact
>
> **Social framework**
> - community impact
> - interest group impact
> - community values
> - social justice principles
> - cultural heritage impact
>
> **Environmental framework**
> - environmental impact analysis
> - ecologically sustainable development principles
> - environmental quality
> - habitat preservation
> - sound management of natural resources
>
> **Legal framework**
> - constitutionality
> - head of power
> - fundamental legislative principles
> - certainty, equality and fairness of the law
> - accessibility to the law
> - enforceability of the policy
>
> **Political framework**
> - consistency with governing party principles and policies
> - consultation with political advisers
> - agreement among policy elites

- discussions with experts within and outside government
- consultation with clients.

The search phase identifies possible options. It also narrows down the possibilities, compressing the potential universe of responses into those choices judged most likely to meet the objectives of decision makers. This judgement is inevitably subjective, and so requires supporting argument and evidence.

In many (but not all) policy areas it is possible to model the consequences of a particular course of action. Models assist comparison of options. Modelling is often strongest when dealing with financial or technical information and at its least effective when trying to calculate the social or political consequences of an option. Governments can model the cost of a new road, the likely usage and the environmental consequences of choosing one route over others. Despite sophisticated local consultation programs and social impact studies, calculating the community response (and subsequent political fallout) remains less reliable.

Providing models — or at least logical arguments — for each option is an important discipline on policy analysts. The requirement to model consequences ensures explicit statements about causation, with assumptions spelled out and reliability specified.

### Solutions

Finally, robust policy analysis should point to potential courses of action. Some problems have a single solution, but most can be addressed in various ways depending on resources and enthusiasm. The product of a policy analysis is usually a briefing paper or report following the steps in analysis — that is, it formulates the problem, establishes objectives, identifies parameters, states alternatives and concludes with one or more recommendations.

Such recommendations should be accompanied by a comparison and, if appropriate, an 'on balance' finding for one choice over others. Ministers will not feel bound by bureaucratic findings, but at least they know how a professional policy analysis has dissected the issue and weighed the alternatives.

If the choices on offer are unpalatable, politicians may seek further information or change some aspect of the equation;

often we need to see options to become certain of our objectives. So policy analysts are reconciled to iteration, to reworking the material in the search for workable choices.

## The analyst's toolkit

Many tools are available for policy analysis. Here we describe the major frameworks commonly used by policy analysts. No policy professional will possess all the expertise identified in these frameworks. This emphasises the need for policy advisers to call on the expertise of others, and to draw a breadth of teamwork advice into their work. This collegiate approach exposes assumptions to scrutiny and tests them. This is a significant step toward building a robust policy, a policy that can engage the real world in the way decision makers seek.

The most fundamental of all analysis takes place in the substantive context of the policy itself. Educational, economic, health, agricultural and legal issues each require focus from relevant policy professionals, who should bring substantive experience to bear on the matter, and who can advise on secondary issues such as *transaction costs* associated with a policy choice. For example, if the policy will alienate a significant group, its opposition may result in financial or legal impediments that bring the option undone, or that need to be accommodated by incorporating effective dispute management strategies within the policy.

## Economic framework

The dominant analytic hegemony of our times is clearly economic. Much public debate is about economic and financial management, so governments need continuing advice on economic and budgeting policy choices. Accordingly, many government initiatives are framed through the perspective of analytical tools based on economic models. These are outlined in Table 5.1. These models in turn influence the major policy instruments used by government. Table 5.2 indicates how economic policy objectives are translated into public sector initiatives, all designed to reduce the scope and outlays of government.

Yet policy analysis is more than budget and various indexes of economics; there are great dangers in analysing a problem solely in economic terms. Social, environmental, legal and political perspectives are also of crucial importance.

**Table 5.1** Economic analysis tools

| Cost-benefit analysis | Cost-effective analysis | Opportunity cost |
|---|---|---|
| Cost-benefit analysis measures whether a policy has economic benefits for the society. It allows comparison of options to determine which will produce the greatest economic benefit. It does so by using dollars as a measurement of policy proposals. Policy makers can then explore the cost to benefit ratio of alternatives.<br><br>Cost-benefit analysis requires significant technical skills, and important subjective judgements about the discount rate to be applied. The discount rate equates present values with future costs and benefits: set too high and future benefit becomes unimportant compared with immediate cost; set too low, and government may waste resources chasing the future, losing the prospect of other, immediate gains: see 'opportunity cost' in this table.<br><br>There is a substantial literature on cost-benefit analysis, much of it hostile to the technique. Critics observe the difficulties of rendering some intangible benefits, such as the aesthetics of an unspoiled wilderness, in dollar terms. They question the emphasis on efficiency as the key criterion for evaluation compared with equity, equality or justice (Anderson, 1994:256).<br><br>Though clearly of limited applicability, the utility of cost-benefit analysis should not be underestimated. Many public problems are open to cost-benefit studies, and foolish decisions can be avoided if simple cost and benefit data are made available. Cost-benefit analysis is not a substitute for political decision making, but it can provide important evidence to inform better those who must choose between alternatives. | Cost-effectiveness is a variation on cost-benefit analysis. It recognises that not all options can be compared. The relative merits of a dam versus an untouched natural river cannot be decided by assigning dollar amounts to each. Yet decision makers need to know whether the options are viable in their own terms.<br><br>Cost-effectiveness analysis examines the merits of a particular proposal. It measures the costs of a policy proposal against the expected benefits in traditional financial terms, the likely return on investment by government. Through cost-effectiveness analysis, decision makers can learn whether a given option will achieve its goals efficiently (Weimar and Vining, 1992:221).<br><br>The results of cost-effectiveness studies can then be compared — if not directly, then against objectives set by government. Cabinet may decide, for example, to spend $20 million on new drought relief programs. A cost-effectiveness analysis will help identify the policy option that gains the most for the available cash.<br><br>Alternatively, cabinet may decide on rural adjustment, such as assisting small-scale farmers and their families to leave their farms and learn new skills for alternative occupations. The farms are thus available for integration into larger-scale, and more efficient, enterprises. Applying a cost-effectiveness test to the options may indicate which alternative will achieve the required outcome for the minimum cost.<br><br>As with cost-benefit analysis, there are limits to applicability. Not all benefits can be measured, nor all costs anticipated. Producing a benefit at the lowest cost may conflict with other goals such as providing employment opportunities. Yet cost-effectiveness analysis can provide important information to inform decision making. | Opportunity cost is a necessary reminder for decision makers that in buying one thing they must forego another. A decision to fund A is also a decision not to fund B (though perhaps not recognised as such).<br><br>Politicians are familiar with the calculus of budgeting — a submarine purchased is a new dam, hospital or school that cannot be built. Economists have developed ways to model opportunity cost, understood as the value placed on the best alternative that must be foregone.<br><br>More difficult to comprehend is the cost of *not* taking action. Yet if government decides against construction of a dam, it should be possible to estimate the subsequent losses to the economy. Government knows how much it saves, but also how much is lost in the long term. The net benefit (or cost) becomes the real measure of the policy option.<br><br>As with cost-benefit analysis, there is subjectivity hidden in the apparently technical certainty of opportunity cost measurement. The approach requires policy analysts to model a best alternative that never happened.<br><br>Still, the opportunity cost concept provides some rigour when making choices, because it provides information about the full cost — not just the cash required up front — of a course of action. |

**Table 5.2** Current Australian public sector initiatives based on economic objectives

**National Competition Policy**

NCP is a national template aiming to remove unnecessary barriers to commercial competitiveness, such as restrictive licensing schemes. Within the public sector, NCP opens up government monopoly for competition. The schedule agreed between the Commonwealth and states imposes a phased program to improve performance by public sector utilities and local government authorities.

Among the related components of NCP are mutual recognition laws, which provide validity for qualifications across Australia, so that a lawyer trained in one jurisdiction can practise in other states or territories. The same laws also facilitate interstate trade in goods and services. As with NCP generally, the objective is to ensure efficiency through competition across national markets.

**Competitive neutrality and commercialisation**

Close relatives of NCP, competitive neutrality and commercialisation aim to ensure the management of government does not distort the market. Thus government entities are to be treated in ways equivalent to private sector participants. They will be structured along commercial lines, subject to equivalent tax regimes, and required to meet the performance, accountability and dividend expectations applicable to companies. The objective is to improve their competitiveness and reduce bureaucratic 'distortions' of decision making.

**Regulatory impact**

Legislation about economic activity carries costs, frequently borne by the business sector. Regulatory impact studies examine such costs and typically apply cost-benefit methods, to assess the need for adjustment or removal of the regulation.

**Reduced outlays**

Governments at all levels have expressed their intention to reduce overall outlays and, in particular, to diminish debt. Less debt frees money currently committed to debt repayment, and some economists argue (though the evidence is equivocal) that lower public sector borrowing will reduce pressure on interest rates. This policy has encouraged the sale of many government assets, budget cuts to remaining operations and a reduction in the services and employment offered by government.

**Competitive Service Delivery**

To ensure efficiencies in public funded programs, governments are promoting Competitive Service Delivery (CSD). Government agencies compete for contracts to deliver a service, or the service is outsourced entirely and awarded on a regular basis to private providers through a tender process. CSD has been applied to many areas of social policy provision, including domiciliary services, labour market programs and even forms processing.

## Social framework

Analysing policy issues and options from a social perspective recognises dimensions that are difficult or impossible to accommodate in the economic framework.

The analyst is challenged by the consequences an option may have for specific sectors, such as women, indigenous Australians, rural communities, people whose first language in not English, people with mobility problems and poor people. Where these groups are not the policy's target, the options are examined in terms of how each will affect the relevant social sector, and whether unintended impacts can be avoided.

'Social infrastructure', the institutions and physical resources through which social programs are delivered, is also important. A program to rationalise, say, local post offices, can have an important impact because of the many ways a community uses this resource.

Analysts often find the 'social justice principles' useful to anchor their analysis of an issue or options. These principles are —

- *Rights.* Does the policy protect or advance individual rights, and educate about social obligations?
- *Equity.* Have interested community groups and individuals been identified and empowered in the policy process? How does each option affect them?
- *Participation.* Full participation in society is a goal of social policy. Thus options are examined in terms of their impact on people's ability to participate, and the resources they need. This is especially true of those who traditionally lack resources through distance, poverty, lack of social institutions validating their participation, or poor language or numeracy skills
- *Access.* Individuals need access to social services. Well structured access allows the service provider to respond more effectively to the needs and expectations of the target groups.

## Environmental framework

Policy options may affect the environment, especially if considering approval for a major project. Analysis must therefore cover not just the economic feasibility of a proposal, but the potential impact on the environment.

It may be good economics to build a third or even fourth runway to manage Sydney air traffic volumes, but what does such a proposal mean for the environment? The environmental impact study is the major tool for answering this question.

Environment is not just land, air and water pollution, or pollution by noise and light. *Biodiversity* must also be considered, bringing specifics of plant and animal habitat into the analyst's frame.

The idea of *ecological sustainability* is also important. Human activity will affect the world around us. The idea behind ecological sustainability is that our activities should be structured in a way that allows regeneration and preservation of the ecology. Other important considerations for environmental policy are *habitat preservation* and *environmental quality*. All these considerations will be incorporated in a well structured environmental impact study.

*Natural resource management* has emerged as another key concern over recent years, with emphasis being placed not only on soil, water, forests and fisheries, but on the interaction that runs to environmentally sensitive areas, such as river catchments.

## Legal framework

Modern notions of government are founded on the resources available to fund programs, employ staff and build infrastructure. More traditional descriptions of the body politic start with the idea of power, exercised by the parliament in the form of law making.

Many policies require legislation to give them effect, and all policies take place in a legal context, because governments are themselves subject to the rule of law.

Fundamental law, the constitutions of the Commonwealth, the states and the territories, describe the limits of governmental power. For example, the Commonwealth may possess the most powerful parliament in our federation, but it is unable to make laws that discriminate on the basis of religion, because the Commonwealth Constitution prohibits it from doing so. States may wish to protect their markets by imposing excises, but this option is not constitutionally open.

As well as a constitution, each jurisdiction in Australia has laws of general application, setting certain requirements on

---

**Table 5.3 Fundamental legislative principles**

**Parliament**
- clarity and precision of legislation
- limiting delegations to make legislation
- parliamentary scrutiny of delegated legislation
- reservation to parliament of power to amend acts
- adequacy of the head of power to make subordinate legislation
- subordinate legislation's consistency with its principal legislation
- appropriateness of subordinate legislation
- subdelegation of power under subordinate legislation only in certain circumstances.

**Individual rights and liberties**
- sufficient definition and provision for review of administrative power
- consistency with the principles of natural justice
- appropriateness of delegation of administrative power
- not reversing the onus of proof in criminal proceedings
- judicial supervision by warrant of powers of entry, search and seizure
- protection from self-incrimination
- retrospective laws
- immunity from prosecution
- fair compensation for compulsory acquisition of property
- regard to Aboriginal tradition and Torres Strait Islander custom.

> The decision maker almost always has information and insight not available to the analyst. Decision makers and political leaders are likely to be keenly aware of the constraints that the context imposes, which must be taken into account in formulating policy. Such constraints are not always evident to the professional analyst …
>
> Edward Quade, 1982:59–60

the policy process. For example, there are laws requiring the auditing of public funds. Policy officers must be aware of such laws when recommending policy options, and ensure any program design conforms with government accountability obligations. Similarly, each jurisdiction has a framework of criminal law, and myriad requirements covering employment, building and other matters. Decision makers must be confident options meet the principles in these laws, but need not specify all the relevant legislation when offering policy advice.

There are also legal principles that apply when developing a legislative proposal for a policy option. As one example, the Queensland parliament stated these fundamental legislative principles in its *Legislative Standards Act* 1992, shown in Table 5.3.

Some of the other analytic frameworks need to be understood in their legal context, too. For example, the economics of competition policies are implemented in a complex legal framework, including the trade practice and fair dealing laws. Social policy manifests itself in laws such as those prohibiting discriminatory behaviour and laws about social order.

## Political analysis

Political analysis of options takes place in the political domain, and is not the task of the policy analyst employed in a government body. Politics is nonetheless fundamental to policy analysis. Good advice is sensitive to the policy goals of a government, without necessarily seeing these as optimal. The policy analyst's role is to ensure political input is made at appropriate times during the analysis stage of policy development, and that policy choices show awareness of the governing party's principles and platform.

## Agreement: an analytic tool

American economist Charles Lindblom proposes a very different method for testing policy options — agreement. Lindblom's (1959, 1965) influential work on incrementalism began as a critique of the rational comprehensive model. Lindblom observed that ends and means in policy making are rarely clear. Often our objectives are defined by available resources, or shift as we learn more about the problem. Real and lasting solutions are rare; most problems receive only amelioration until they fade from view or are superseded. The urgent tends to crowd out the important.

> Policy making is a process of successive approximation to some desired objective in which what is desired itself continues to change under reconsideration.
>
> Charles Lindblom, 1959:86

Further, Lindblom noted, there is never enough time or energy to conduct a comprehensive search for alternatives. We do not address each new problem by starting from first principles. Policy makers prefer 'successive limited comparisons' with current practice, modifying existing programs to deal with new issues. Sometimes these modifications are tested through pilot programs. Policy proceeds by small experiments to see if familiar responses can resolve an emerging problem.

What, then, is the test of a good policy? Not a strong cost-benefit ratio or specification of lost opportunities, argues Lindblom, but agreement. A successful policy is one which commands consensus among policy makers and interest groups. Table 5.4 compares an incrementalism approach with an ideally rational policy process.

In this view, policy makers build up a bank of knowledge about a policy area, and programs to match. This makes them reluctant to move suddenly 'in an entirely different direction'; better to experiment with small changes than to seek major policy departures (Hayes, 1992:18). An inherent conservatism is built into the policy process.

Like the rational comprehensive model it sought to displace, incrementalism has many critics. Small steps may produce only circular movement. Agreement among elites is no guarantee that broader social interests are being served by a policy. Major problems facing society may need a radical push, not an incremental approach.

**Table 5.4** Two models of policy analysis

| Rational policy making | Incrementalist |
| --- | --- |
| Clarification of values or objectives distinct from and usually prerequisite to empirical analysis of alternative policies | Selection of value goals and empirical analysis of the needed action are not distinct but are closely intertwined |
| Policy formulation is therefore approached through means–end analysis: first the ends are isolated, then the means to achieve them are sought | Since ends and means are not distinct, means–end analysis is often inappropriate or limited |
| The test of a 'good' policy is that it can be shown to be the most appropriate means to desired ends | The test of a 'good' policy is typically that various analysts find themselves agreeing on a policy (without their agreeing that it is the most appropriate means to an agreed objective) |
| Analysis is comprehensive.<br>Every important relevant factor is taken into account | Analysis is limited drastically —<br>• important possible outcomes are neglected<br>• important alternative potential policies are neglected<br>• important affected values are neglected |
| Theory is often relied upon heavily | A succession of comparisons greatly reduces or eliminates reliance on theory |

(Source: Lindblom, 1959:81)

**Practical hints for presenting policy advice**
- consider the nature of the times (e.g. electoral cycles, issue agendas)
- ensure you understand ministerial and/or senior management requirements
- network and consult about ideas and/or proposals
- clarify whether the minister's office should be involved. If unsure how to proceed, advise senior management or the minister's office
- when determining the key components of policy advice (e.g. objectives, scope, costing, implications) ensure administrative logics take account of political sensitivities; do not present purely partisan advice
- consider timing and/or alert senior management to timing issues
- briefs to ministers may become early drafts for cabinet submissions. Consider the requirements of cabinet when briefing ministers
- written and oral advice must be succinct, coherent, clear and support well-reasoned recommendations
- competently assess the policy's life. Is it a closing decision, a policy with limited life or an open ended proposal?
- anticipate future needs/requirements.

Source: John Wanna et al., 1994:2.14

Yet, despite these and other complaints, incrementalism probably most accurately describes how policy making proceeds. It stresses the expertise of bureaucrats and the economy of working out from familiar programs. To use only incrementalism would be as serious a mistake as relying too heavily on cost-benefit or cost-effectiveness analyses to make decisions; but sometimes, as Lindblom suggests, policy analysts must use judgement about how much time and thought to invest in a problem. The quick and rough calculations of incrementalism may be the most effective way to proceed.

## Why analysis?

Policy issues are usually complex and costly to address. The process of analysis ensures decision makers are well informed, and can chose from an array of potential solutions, each explored thoroughly.

Through analysis we give shape to a problem — establishing its characteristics, drawing boundaries, bringing crucial variables into clear relief. Analysis allows a policy professional to 'frame' an issue, stating it in terms that make the problem open to possible policy approaches.

When solutions are not obvious, analysts learn to reframe the question, stating the problems in different ways to get a broader sense of the question. Often the initial presentation of an issue constrains the range of options too tightly. Sometimes, too, a problem is first presented in terms of a solution. 'We need to amend the Act and impose a night time flight curfew,' laments one person. 'Money is needed to build a new airport,' cries another. Each is proposing a solution, rather than stating the problem in policy terms.

The analyst starts with a problem and a policy objective, then expands and contracts the dimensions of the issue by asking questions, gathering and analysing data, seeking opinions and views. The aim is to frame an issue in terms that make it intelligible to others, and open to the analytic tools available to policy professionals.

Discussions of technique in policy analysis tend to imply a rational and sequential process. Experience, however, tells policy analysts to expect iteration. As problems are defined and redefined, solution parameters shift and objectives waver. This is not a counsel of despair, just a warning that the way of policy analysis rarely runs smooth.

Underlying policy analysis is judgement. Some problems deserve sustained attention from teams, with full modelling and careful consideration of all variables. Others can be resolved quickly, with minimal search for alternatives. There is no magic rule that distinguishes one type of policy from the other.

Eminent practitioners discussing policy analysis usually conclude with a plea for judgement — that indefinable mix of experience and intelligence said to guide good policy analysts. One might also call for attention to ethical scruples, in particular the importance of objectivity both when selecting and presenting options. The potential conflict between the two (judgement requiring subjectivity, ethics preferring impartiality) is a paradox of professional life (see Waller, 1996). Good policy analysis presents options without spin, but it does not present all options, only those judged most likely to meet stated objectives.

# Chapter 6
# Policy Instruments

> **Snapshot**
>
> Policy instruments are the means governments use to achieve their ends.
>
> There are broadly four types of policy instrument available —
> - advocacy — arguing a case; informing
> - money — using spending and taxing powers
> - government action — delivering services
> - law — using legislative power.
>
> Good policy advice relies on choosing the right instrument for the problem at hand.

The excitement and bustle of politics, and the technical judgement of policy advice must yield eventually to the more measured process of turning ideas into reality if a policy is to take effect in the world. An idea means nothing if it cannot be converted into practical application. This chapter is concerned with that conversion, and the range of 'policy instruments' available to government to achieve its ends.

Governments influence what happens in society through their repertoire of policy instruments. If results are the *ends* of the policy process, instruments are the *means* — the programs, staffing, budgets, organisations, campaigns and laws giving effect to policy decisions.

The policy cycle asks policy professionals to consider policy instruments once they are clear about objectives and goals. Analytically, it is important to keep objectives separate from instruments. There may be more than one way to achieve the same goal, and some means carry too high political costs.

In Britain, for example, the conservative government of Margaret Thatcher was committed to reform of local government financing. Despite warnings from cabinet colleagues, the prime minister chose a poll tax as an instrument to achieve this objective. The subsequent urban riots, and the clear unworkability of the scheme, were significant factors in her downfall as prime minister. Mrs Thatcher's successor readily found less provocative instruments to pursue the same goal.

The temptation to call on an instrument from the repertoire before analysing fully the nature of the issue is also risky for the policy analyst. The means becomes the end; the instrument, a solution in search of a problem. Experience suggests that choosing the approach at once, and only analysing the problem later, is more common than might be expected — especially with legislation as a first resort.

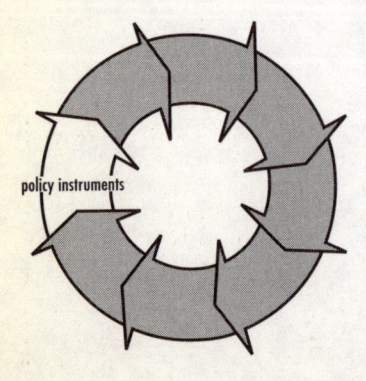

All instruments have strengths and weakness. As with selection of options, professional judgement is required when advising on choices. Decision makers need to know whether policy options are viable, and the comparative merits of alternative approaches.

## Classifying policy instruments

Arguments over typologies may seem irrelevant to the main game of making public policy — a sport for professors. Yet, as Hood (1983) argues, government options are limited by available instruments. Great policy ideas are of little use without appropriate means. Knowledge about the range of choice is therefore essential.

No typology captures fully the complexity of policy instrument choice but categories are important. They help make sense of various government actions. They display the array of instrument choice and draw attention to alternative ways of achieving goals.

There are myriad policy instruments, from the very broad to the highly specific. An early study of economic policy identified some 64 different instruments in that one field alone (Howlett and Ramesh, 1995:81). Economic writings warn that instruments must be matched precisely to objectives — even though governments inevitably have more objectives than available instruments.

Recent research suggests important trends in policy instrument choice. Canadians Atkinson and Nigol (1989:111) note that 'governments, under pressure to restrain expenditures, have sought to employ less obtrusive means of intervention'. Further, 'politicians prefer to employ the least coercive instruments possible'. Thus the more coercive regulation, taxation and public ownership approaches are no longer politically favoured.

There is also movement away from law toward other forms of policy instrument. In the Australian context, the strengthening of the parliamentary committee systems, and parliamentary scrutiny of legislation committees in particular, has fostered this bias towards less intrusive instruments.

New typologies of policy instruments are emerging, categorising according to the role of government in a policy area. Howlett and Ramesh (1995:81ff) identify three key types of policy instrument —

---

**What is a policy instrument?**

Policy instruments are the methods used to achieve policy objectives.

*Poor instrument choice.* A public education program about alternative crops will have little effect on illegal marijuana production. Increased criminal penalties have been shown also in an overwhelming number of criminological studies to have little effect on crime rates.

*Multiple instruments.* The Sydney air traffic example employs a wide range of instruments — **law:** regulation of aircraft noise levels and airport curfews; **money:** cash transfers to subsidise noise insulation of affected houses; increased carrying capacity (the third runway) to reduce landing stacks; **advocacy:** feasibility studies of an extra airport to shift the noise away from the populated areas while expanding capacity; community consultative groups; **action:** Air Services Australia instructed to review operating procedures and develop a long term plan.

Even simple policy proposals may use multiple instruments. Addressing speeding by motorists might require legislative amendments to allow use of new speed detection equipment plus increased penalties, coupled with public announcements and education programs about the change.

> Christopher Hood (1983: 4–6) identifies four broad classes of policy instruments:
> - 'nodality' — using information to influence public behaviour
> - 'treasure' — use of government money or resources to shape actions
> - 'authority' — legal or official powers
> - 'organisations' — policies delivered by government agencies.

- 'voluntary' instruments involve little role for government beyond advocacy and persuasion; typical targets include families, voluntary organisations and private markets

- 'mixed' instruments include a greater role for the state, and include information and exhortation, subsidies, auction of property rights and tax and user chargers

- finally, 'compulsory' instruments include regulation, public enterprises and direct provision of services.

## Australian policy instruments

In a federal system, policy instruments differ across jurisdictions. The Commonwealth has powers and responsibilities not open to the states, and exclusive access to some important revenue streams.

Commonwealth powers have grown over the decades, aided by successive centralising governments, High Court support of Commonwealth legislation and, very occasionally, successful referenda. The Commonwealth has come to dominate the federation, particularly in financial matters. States might spend large amounts on education, transport and health, but they rely on the Commonwealth for most of their income, creating a 'vertical fiscal imbalance'.

This financial dependency allows the Commonwealth, through 'tied grants', to dictate policy in areas nominally the responsibility of states.

Local government is the silent partner in the division of powers, not being mentioned in the Constitution. It draws authority from state acts. Closer links between the federal government and the regions over recent years raise the possibility that local government will eventually, like the states, become financially dependent on the Commonwealth.

The federal division of powers is a major constraint on selection of policy instruments in an Australian setting. The constitution, and subsequent inter-governmental financial arrangements, temper any typology of policy instrument types, for only a limited range of approaches are available to state and local government.

Drawing on Hood (1983), we identify four common types of policy instrument used in Australia —

> ... governments can achieve their policy goals in a number of ways. Students of policy instruments have argued that the means chosen affect not only the success or failure of policies, but also the political fortunes of decision makers.
>
> Michael Atkinson and Robert Nigol, 1989:107

- policy through *advocacy* — educating or persuading, using information available to government
- policy through *money* — using spending and taxing powers to shape activity beyond government
- policy through direct *government action* — delivering services through public agencies
- policy through *law* — legislation, regulation and official authority.

We can then map these policy instruments against the Australian division of powers.

## Policy through advocacy

Advocacy instruments argue a case rather than force a result. Often they draw government into working closely with interest groups. Anti-smoking campaigns, for example, bring together state and federal departments of health, the Heart Foundation and the Australian Medical Association.

Such consultation is a growing feature of policy formation. In some policy areas, government agrees not to impose laws in return for sector agreements about shared objectives (for example, 'self-regulation' by various professions).

**Table 6.1** Policy through advocacy

| Jurisdiction | Instruments | Examples |
| --- | --- | --- |
| Commonwealth | • funding for public education promotional activity<br>• establishment of consultative bodies<br>• ministerial speeches and events to attract publicity for causes and ideas<br>• policy announcement | • publicity campaign to encourage electors to vote<br>• hosting meetings of farm groups to discuss drought policy<br>• ministerial presentation to annual conferences of industry groups<br>• issuing a discussion paper on new vehicle regulations for discussion |
| State | • funding for public education promotional activity<br>• establishment of consultative boards<br>• ministerial speeches and events to attract publicity for causes and ideas<br>• policy announcement | • anti-smoking advertising campaigns<br>• meeting with Ethnic Communities Council<br>• graduation speech by Education Minister<br>• launching a green paper on land clearing for consultation |
| Local government | • promotion of council initiatives through suburban newspapers<br>• establishment of consultative bodies | • 'town meeting' initiatives to discuss local planning and development issues<br>• financial support for regional economic development committees |

## Policy through money

Governments have multiple objectives when making fiscal decisions. At the broadest level, they hope to influence the economy, though deregulation of financial markets and a reduction in tariffs have diminished greatly the capacity of the Commonwealth to control macro-economic outcomes.

A second objective for government is to ensure sufficient revenue. Tax policy must strike a balance between encouraging enterprise and funding government programs. People want services, but are often reluctant to pay. Tax increases are seen politically as being unpopular, and governments often struggle to balance their books.

Governments also use resources to achieve outcomes. Tax dollars fund industry development, schools, universities and other instruments of government policy. Groups and institutions outside government spend much time lobbying for money, arguing about the contribution they can make if appropriately funded.

**Table 6.2** Policy through money

| Jurisdiction | Instruments | Examples |
|---|---|---|
| Commonwealth | • fiscal powers to shape macro economic outcomes<br>• taxing powers on individuals, organisations and businesses<br>• incentive payments for private sector activity<br>• grants programs for state activity | • cutting government spending to reduce public sector indebtedness<br>• imposing higher levels of excise on luxury goods<br>• research and development grants for new industries<br>• Commonwealth payments to private schools |
| State | • limited taxing powers on land, financial transactions, gambling, levies and fines<br>• incentives to attract major industrial, commercial and tourism developments<br>• infrastructure spending for exonomic development | • increase in pay-roll tax thresholds to attract business<br>• reduction in electricity tariffs or provision of cheap land in return for investment<br>• construction of new rail and port facilities |
| Local government | • rates, levies and limited other income sources<br>• user-charging for council facilities<br>• limited capacity to offer financial incentives for local government<br>• attraction of business sponsorship to support local activities | • introduction of a 'green levy' on households to fund nature reserve purchases<br>• charges on building plan approvals, and for inspection of property<br>• finding a company to sponsor a new art exhibition |

## Policy through government action

While much money held by government is used for transfer payments — to other levels of government, to private organisations, to individuals — a significant proportion is invested in public sector programs and agencies.

Such public sector activities are considered in a budget round, and settled by cabinet before presentation to parliament. Governments deliver services through the public sector, accounting for expenditure through annual reports and parliamentary scrutiny. Though government influences much in society, our main points of contact are often with such services, from transport to hospitals.

At all levels of government, there is movement away from direct government action. Governments choose to 'contract out' functions, relying on private providers who deliver services to a standard specified in a contract. As a result, the size of the public sector is diminishing in most jurisdictions, even though the reach and scope of government remains unchanged. Gary Sturgess (1996) describes this trend as 'virtual government', in which the public service funds, but does not deliver, services traditionally associated with government.

**Table 6.3** Policy through government action

| Jurisdiction | Instruments | Examples |
| --- | --- | --- |
| Commonwealth | - cabinet decisions<br>- creation of new institutions<br>- public service programs<br>- funding for service provision by statutory bodies or non-government agencies<br>- administrative decisions | - allocation of budget to agencies<br>- universal health coverage through Medicare<br>- social security services and offices<br><br>- guidelines on dealing with sexual harassment in public sector workplaces |
| State | - cabinet decisions<br>- creation of new institutions<br>- public service programs<br>- funding for service provision by statutory bodies or non-government agencies<br>- administrative decisions | - new programs for rural communities<br>- establishment of an Environmental Protection Agency<br>- schools, hospitals, rail services, road construction<br><br>- guidelines governing promotions within the public service |
| Local government | - service delivery either by council or through contractors<br>- cultural services | - waste disposal, sewerage, curbing and guttering<br>- libraries, child care facilities, meeting rooms |

## Policy through law

The law is the traditional instrument of government policy, and the final guarantee that policy intent can be translated into action.

Laws can facilitate, allowing a course of action, or coerce, requiring or prohibiting certain behaviour. In passing laws, parliament empowers the government to act and provides for enforcement through the police and courts. Laws are also binding on government, and many impose specific and unique obligations on the political, policy and administrative domains. Freedom of information legislation, for example, makes many government deliberations open to public scrutiny.

Laws establish a framework for government action, but much of the detail is contained in regulations — delegated legislation authorised by an act and implemented by officials. Delegated legislation includes regulations, by-laws and ordinances. Local governments, for example, make by-laws, using the authority delegated to them by state government legislation.

To interpret this universe of laws requires courts and quasi-judicial bodies such as the Human Rights and Equal Opportunity Commission and literally hundreds of administrative appeals tribunals. Such legal bodies are

**Table 6.4** Policy through law

| Jurisdiction | Instruments | Examples |
|---|---|---|
| Commonwealth | • legislation<br>• subordinate legislation (regulation)<br>• parliamentary resolution<br>• administrative acts | • *Income Tax Assessment Act*<br>• regulations governing competition<br>• affirmation of a non-discriminatory immigration policy<br>• visa application determination |
| State | • legislation<br>• subordinate legislation (regulation)<br>• parliamentary resolution<br>• administrative acts | • *Anti-Discrimination Act*<br>• Criminal Code<br>• regulations governing fishing in national parks<br>• creation of a parliamentary committee<br>• hotel licence granted |
| Local government | • zoning and development approval powers<br>• town planning regulations<br>• building approvals | • zoning land for residential development<br>• rejecting a building approval as inconsistent with the character of an area |

zealous about their right to make independent judgments, even though they are funded by government.

## Choosing a policy instrument

The criteria for selecting the best policy instrument in given circumstances involve a combination of technical efficiency and political nous. Some simple questions help guide the choice —

- *appropriateness* — is this a reasonable way of proceeding in this policy area?
- *efficiency* — will this instrument be cost-effective?
- *effectiveness* — can this instrument get the job done?
- *equity* — are the likely consequences fair?
- *workability* — is the instrument simple and robust, and can it be implemented?

The choice of policy instruments matters. It is the link between an objective and its attainment. The right instrument will be appropriate, efficient, effective, equitable and workable.

Like much else in the policy cycle, judgement as well as science is required to select the best available instrument. As Hood (1983:163) notes, however skilfully policy instruments are used they do not enable government 'to shape the world outside in any way that it likes. There are some inherent limitations.' The simple application of a government toolkit cannot solve 'wicked problems', nor poorly structured issues. Policy instruments need to be backed by sufficient authority and money, and chosen in a framework of rigorous thinking about ends as well as means.

Some policy objectives are simply beyond government. The surrender of economic controls over the economy, for example, may have long-term benefits for growth and competitiveness, but it means government has only limited ability to influence important (and highly politically sensitive) variables such as inflation or interest rates.

It is imperative, then, to choose the right policy instrument. But it is equally important to be plain-spoken when no such instrument exists. Good tools cannot rescue bad policy.

> ... governments in the future — and citizens making demands on those governments — may need to become more aware of what is in government's tool-box in order to develop a better understanding of the possibilities and limitations of what government can do.
> ... success in government, in the future as in the past, will depend on its ability to apply a relatively fixed set of basic tools imaginatively to each new situation as it arises.
> Christopher Hood, 1983:168.

> If the only tool you have is a hammer, soon every problem begins to look like a nail.
> Proverb

# Chapter 7
# Consultation

**Snapshot**
Consultation takes place throughout the policy cycle. However, as policy problems are analysed and options emerge, government may wish to test its choice with a wider community. The main tool for this testing is consultation.

The defining feature of democracy is free, fair elections, through which citizens periodically participate in government. Yet, increasingly, citizens want a say between elections on choices affecting their community. Governments are learning to include participation in the policy cycle.

Whereas secrecy was once the hallmark of the political and policy domains alike, community expectations have shifted. Groups outside government expect involvement in decision making. The legitimacy of much public policy now rests on an exchange between citizens and their government. Public servants and politicians must find ways to discuss with relevant communities of interest and draw them into the policy process, yet avoid unreasonable delays or simple vetoing by unrepresentative groups.

## The role of consultation

The pressure on governments to consult about public policy is considerable, and unlikely to diminish. New forms of accountability, such as developments in administrative law, encourage consultation as a phase within the public policy cycle. Seeking a viewpoint from those affected by a policy decision is sometimes a legal requirement, and often just smart policy making.

A consultative process offers policy makers a way to structure debate, and to develop a solution more likely to 'stick' because it reflects the realities of the problem and the competing interests of those involved.

However, consultation carries costs, especially expense and delays inherent in managing a large consultation exercise, and the risk of debate dominated by committed but unrepresentative voices.

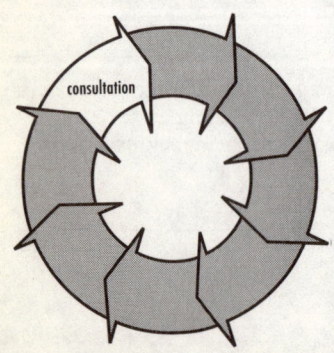

While consultation is valued by government for addressing legitimacy problems over contentious decisions, consultation has its own legitimacy issues (Davis, 1996:16). Who can claim a voice in consultation? If government alone decides, it risks imposing its preferences and so undermining the benefits of consultation. If self-appointed spokespersons for 'the public interest' dominate the process, the results may not accurately reflect community feeling.

There are problems weighting differing voices. Access to the consultation process and capacity to state a case are seldom distributed evenly. It is always easier to deal with interest groups who can speak authoritatively for their membership. Yet there is a risk such groups will eclipse other, less organised, interests, or fail their members and not be representative at all.

Deciding whether to use consultation requires analysis of the costs and benefits, based on the type of decision and the value of sharing the choice with interested individuals and groups. Formal cost-benefit studies may sometimes be appropriate. However, a consultation strategy is driven largely by the nature of the problem at hand. Deciding when to consult (or whether to consult at all) is as much political judgement as a procedural issue.

Consulting serves specific purposes, but it also serves as a reflection of values, of a desire to be open and transparent. Decisions about public participation in decision making need to be made in a dialogue about the technical requirements of public service advisers and the political needs of elected officials.

Sometimes it is useful to wonder about how a decision reached in isolation might look as tomorrow's headline, and reflect again whether some consultation might be warranted. Of course consultation can be frustrating too, adding time to already difficult processes, and shifting control away from ministers and bureaucrats to those invited into the policy process.

> Consultation is used by governments for one or more of the following six objectives —
> - supporting democratic values
> - building consensus and political support
> - improving regulatory quality through information collection
> - reducing regulatory costs on enterprises, citizens and administrations
> - quickening responsiveness
> - carrying out strategic agendas.
>
> OECD, 1994:6–9

## Different types of consultation

An OECD study by Shand and Arnberg (1996:21) suggested public involvement in government action can be placed on a continuum, from minimal interaction through to complete cooperation.

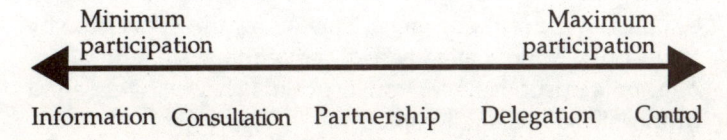

Minimum participation ←──────────────→ Maximum participation

Information   Consultation   Partnership   Delegation   Control

> The degree of group involvement desirable in making a decision depends on the attributes of the core problem; some problems demand more involvement, others less.
> John Thomas, 1990:435

*Information* involves informing people about government policy. An advertising campaign to encourage safer driving — and announce the introduction of speed cameras — is a familiar example of a government information campaign. This is a one-way process, educating the public about some policy initiative and its objectives. It does not allow client input to a choice. (Compare 'advocacy' as a policy instrument in Chapter 6.)

*Consultation* seeks input from individuals and groups to a policy decision. Here consultation involves an exchange, though the decision makers remain in charge of the agenda and outcome. The process may involve surveys, public hearings or, more typically, meetings with interest groups representing various players in the policy arena. The goal is to improve policy, and enhance its acceptability, by taking into account the comments and interests of those likely to be affected. Regulation covering workplace health and safety, for example, is developed in this mode, with regular discussions between government, industry and unions.

*Partnership* hands some control of a decision from decision makers to the public. In this mode, clients can do more than just express opinion. They have some say over policy content, working in cooperation with decision makers. Often this is achieved through consultation structures, with clients and experts sitting on advisory boards, helping shape policy and its implementation. Many welfare services, for example, use advisory boards of clients and public servants to decide priorities within the government's overall framework.

> The literature on consultation includes all the following techniques —
> - public information campaigns
> - focus groups
> - surveys — key informants, clients and citizens
> - circulation of proposals for written comment
> - advisory committees
> - interest group meetings
> - town hall meetings
> - public hearings
> - public inquiries
> - citizens advisory committees
> - impact assessment studies
> - policy communities
> - referenda.

*Delegation* hands control of the policy agenda to an outside group. In Australia the commission of inquiry is a familiar instrument for making policy choices. So too are statutory authorities, keeping government at arm's length from some contentious area. In most states, for example, parole for prisoners is determined by a community board with no direct role for politicians. Fisheries management, a highly fraught matter, is also often handled by a statutory authority. Monetary policy is managed by an independent Reserve Bank.

Finally, it is possible to pass *control* of a policy issue entirely to the public. Section 128 of the Australian Constitution establishes the referendum as a means for direct decision by the people. There have been 20 referenda since federation, offering 42 proposals for constitutional change. Only eight proposals have been accepted.

Referenda can also be used to determine non-constitutional issues, from the choice of national anthem to the introduction of daylight saving and extended trading hours in some states. Popular control of a policy issue is an important way to settle controversial topics in which the policy process is unlikely to reach a satisfactory, or legitimate, resolution.

Another currently popular method for transferring policy control of the more commercial government activities is privatisation. Control here is vested in the shareholders of a new entity rather than the public at large, shifting the policy dynamic from the public domain to the powerful world of large corporations.

## Consultation instruments

With the continuum for consultation options identified, it becomes possible to identify the various instruments that help achieve consultation objectives. These are set out in Table 7.1.

### Information

Information campaigns adopt the standard techniques of marketing. *Surveys* provide data on public opinion. Almost always this work is done outside government, by market research companies competing for government contracts. Companies also provide *focus group research* to test and refine a message. Focus groups bring together people chosen for their demographic characteristics, who discuss a particular issue, view a trial advertisement, or respond to key words and phrases. Such groups indicate how the intended audience will respond to the government's message. Finally, with the research completed, governments use a mix of advertising avenues to present a *public information campaign*.

**Table 7.1** Purpose of consultation and appropriate consultation instruments

| Information | Consultation | Partnership | Delegation | Control |
|---|---|---|---|---|
| • surveys<br>• focus groups<br>• public information campaign | • key contacts<br>• interest groups meetings<br>• town hall meetings<br>• circulation of proposals<br>• public hearings | • advisory committees<br>• policy communities | • public inquiries<br>• impact assessment studies | • referenda<br>• privatisation |

(Source: Davis, 1996:18)

Information campaigns are a necessary, if sometimes controversial, part of governing. Often policy success relies on implementation by the public (as in obeying new laws). But information campaigns are not consultation, since the flow is only one-way. Such campaigns have a role in the policy process, but will not satisfy those looking for more meaningful interaction. A common, traditional instrument for public policy information is the 'white paper'.

## Consultation

The consultation mode seeks to solicit, and respond to, views about a policy proposal from relevant people and groups.

Those who advise and make policy build up contacts with players in their policy area. These *key contacts* become an important conduit for information, both informally, and through representation on advisory boards. Since key contacts may be a limited group, however, policy makers also arrange *interest group meetings* to exchange views on a policy area with those who represent a viewpoint on government action. Should a policy proposal have implications for a community, as in an urban renewal or freeway project, policy makers may also organise *town hall meetings* so the local community can hear about, and express views on, a proposed course of action.

If the constituency is diffuse, or the players too many to allow face to face meetings, government may introduce a more formal consultation process. Many proposed regulations, for example, are made available through *circulation of proposals*. An intention to change a subordinate law is advertised in the press, with a date set for responses. Interested parties can put their case and these are considered in the final policy decision. The discussion paper or 'green paper' is a traditional means of consulting about a policy proposal. Alternatively, a process of *public hearings* is established, in which policy makers listen to points of view and consider the various cases before making recommendations.

Whichever combination of techniques is adopted, the consultation method always involves opportunities for public input. Yet policy makers remain in control of the process and its results. Faced with opposition to a proposal, policy makers may find it wise to withdraw. They are under no obligation, however, to so do. Consultation offers input but not a veto for individuals or interest groups on policy choices.

---

In *Making Equity Planning Work*, Cleveland Planning Commission Director Norman Krumholz and urban planning academic John Forster (1990) describe an ambitious series of programs designed to deal with the mix of urban decay, racism and poverty found in an old industrial city. Krumholz and his team abandoned the traditional approach of carefully formulated rational town planning in favour of a rolling program of consultation over freeway siting, low and moderate income housing, land planning, parks and transit issues. The planning team saw its task as essentially political — to develop plans that won Town Hall and community support, through working with coalitions of interested community groups, developers and local officials. The approach was not without some failures, but provided more than usual participation and agreement across what one observer had previously described as 'the anger that is Cleveland'.

*Partnership*

Partnership strategies draw the community into decision making. The standard mechanism for inclusion is the *advisory committee*. Community representatives on an advisory committee can provide policy makers with direct and unfiltered views. Various OECD studies emphasise the widespread use of such committees as the primary vehicle for consultation (OECD, 1994a). Governments appreciate the two-way exchange provided by committees — greater community input into policy — but also an opportunity for policy makers to explain their approach and objectives.

Over time, advisory committees can become *policy communities* — regular meetings of the key interests in a policy field — with an opportunity to broker agreements (Sabatier and Jenkins-Smith, 1993). Governments see their role as providing a forum for discussions, ensuring the participants are representative of the broader community's interests, and proposing policy ideas that can be debated, modified and adopted with some measure of common support.

Contentious policy areas, such as the environment and industrial relations, particularly suit this form of consultation. Policy communities allow the players to understand each other's concerns and interests, and seek agreements balancing competing interests. In environmental policy, for example, industry needs and conservation goals are brought together, with depth of understanding developing on both sides, while policy makers benefit from both improved information and developing accord on central points. Policy communities can be slow and difficult forums for policy discussion, but they may find resolutions where otherwise only conflict and disagreement prevail.

Representativeness must be carefully considered when consulting through partnership bodies. Can a public housing client or an employee's representative claim to speak for others? Why, when discussing people with disabilities, should one organisation but not another have a voice in the consultation? Governments often address this concern by asking peak bodies to represent their sector.

To assist with consultation, governments sometimes create peak bodies. The Health Consumers Forum, for example, was founded and funded by government to represent consumer interests in various health policy discussions.

---

**Examples of peak bodies**
- Aboriginal and Torres Strait Islander Commission, representing indigenous Australians
- Australian Business Council, representing industry
- Australian Council of Trade Unions, representing workers
- Australian Council of Social Service, representing the welfare sector
- the National Farmers Federation, representing rural producers.

**Examples of public inquiries with policy implications**
- Coombs inquiry into the Australian government administration (1974–75)
- Fitzgerald inquiry into police corruption in Queensland (1987–89)
- Mansfield inquiry into the Australian Broadcasting Corporation (1996)
- Industry Commission inquiry into ecologically sustainable land management (1997).

### Delegation

Delegation aims to shift policy responsibility to an institution or process outside political control. This may be as close as the policy cycle ever comes to an ideal 'rational' process, in which evidence is collected and weighed, and judgement provided with supporting arguments.

*Public inquiries* are a standard feature of Australian policy formulation. They provide an impartial forum to explore an issue and settle on authoritative recommendations (Weller, 1994). Inquiries seek submissions to obtain evidence and views. Public hearings provide opportunities for consultation. Reports typically list the range of arguments and evidence put before the inquiry, indicating the dimensions of the policy debate. Of course, inquiries can also be a way for governments to defer contentious issues. British prime minister Harold Wilson's famous formulation was that royal commissions 'take minutes and waste years'.

The use of *assessment studies* is a more recent style of delegation. Here, governments impose a process on decision making. Proposals for a new tourism development or mine must meet certain threshold standards before government will issue the necessary approval or lease. Independent consultants study the proposal and consult with the local community. Their detailed reports form one important basis for government's decision. Environmental impact studies are the most familiar such form of assessment, and social impact studies are becoming important to policy making (see, for example, Holden and O'Faircheallaigh, 1995; see also Chapter 5 about policy analysis frameworks). Such studies are particularly useful when communities are sharply divided on the merits of a proposal, since the study provides detailed and authoritative data on all aspects of the choice, including the views of interested parties. Assessment studies provide government with grounds for a decision on technical rather than political criteria.

### Control

It is rare in Australia to hand control of an issue directly to the people despite the constitutional provision for referenda.

In principle, referenda could be used to resolve issues that are too fundamental or too contentious for the usual business of politics. Without a controlled approach to consultation, such issues result in non-decisions, reflecting the unwillingness of politicians to tackle very divisive subjects.

---

> The idea of direct democracy proposes a more continuous, active role for citizens. Theorists who call for the implementation of such an idea are proposing much more significant levels of participation than prevail in a representative democracy, through such institutional mechanisms as direct local assemblies or the extensive use of referenda. In contemporary political life such ideas have achieved considerable prominence because of the size, impersonality and power of modern governments, whose elected politicians do not always appear accessible and, in any case, seem to have become dominated by non-elected parts of the governing system, notably bureaucracies.
>
> Martin Painter, 1992:22

Laws about moral issues like abortion, prostitution, euthanasia and same-sex relationships, for example, often have little relation to actual practice. It is easier to leave the old statutes in place — but ignore them — than to open touchy debates to the popular will.

In Australia, citizens have few ways of forcing government to put issues to a vote. The referendum mechanism entrenched in the Commonwealth and most state constitutions can only be activated by parliament. This contrasts with practice in the United States and New Zealand, where forms of citizen initiated referenda allow individuals and groups to propose propositions for ballot. Yet, as Franklin (1992:59) argues, 'reducing all policy questions for voters to a simple yes/no form, is hardly an appropriate method of government or political discussion. Few issues lend themselves to simplification in this way.'

Privatising government activity removes government control, and vests it in the hands of a select group — shareholders. This cuts out potential conflicts of interest between government as trading entity and government as regulator and policy maker. Privately owned and operated airports are not amenable to government's direction, and policy can only be directed by government through regulation or cooperative arrangements with the new owners.

## Designing a consultation process

To avoid the pitfalls of consultation, processes must be tightly structured, with clearly specified terms of reference, time lines and outcomes. This lets parties to the consultation know the process to be followed and keeps the discussion focused (Davis, 1996:22–24).

### Purpose

Policy makers may decide on consultation to —

- improve the quality of policy decisions through access to relevant information and perspectives
- ensure understanding, acceptance and legitimacy of proposed policies
- promote consensus about policy choices
- anticipate challenges to the policy process by providing transparency, accountability and opportunities for participation.

> Most governments have not articulated very clearly their objectives for consultation. This lack of clarity has both good and bad implications. On the one hand, the general acceptance of consultation as inherently desirable, even without clear goals, demonstrates its powerful appeal within modern societies. It is supported by strong and fundamental values that, in some countries, mean that the value of consultation is virtually unquestioned. This encouraging environment makes reform and expansion of consultation easier. On the other hand, the failure to establish clear objectives means that consultation programmes are more likely to be inappropriately designed, inefficient, difficult to evaluate, and disappointing or even disillusioning in results to public and public administrators alike. These kinds of outcomes serve only to discredit consultation efforts.
>
> OECD, 1994:5–6

From the purpose, and the problem to be addressed, flows the appropriate type of consultation.

*Method*
- the resources to be spent on consultation must reflect the nature and significance of the problem to be addressed, and the time available
- most consultation processes use a range of instruments, aiming to limit the inherent biases of any one approach by seeking opinion through a range of different avenues
- agencies should be clear about their objectives. These can range from disseminating information through to consultation, partnership, delegation or control.

*Identifying stakeholders*
- while consultation material may be distributed to those identified by policy makers as relevant interests, there must be avenues for others to self-identify as parties to the consultation process
- barriers such as language, physical and education disadvantage, resources and time may keep some stakeholders from contributing. The mix of consultation methods must address inclusiveness in the process
- it is important to advertise the consultation process, even if most who see the advertisement will choose not to participate.

*Beginning consultation*
- the objectives and parameters of consultation should be clear. Documentation should establish in advance the purpose, process and outputs of the consultation phase
- policy makers must identify the full impact of a proposal so all affected interests understand the issue at stake
- the process of consultation should be transparent throughout
- consultation should begin early enough to permit consideration of comments and suggested alternatives.

*Consulting with individuals and groups*
- policy makers should meet with the main interest groups to discuss their views. The purpose and

---

**Queensland's principles of consultation**

1. Consultation is an essential component of the policy making process.
2. Effective consultation should occur early and throughout the policy process.
3. Each consultation needs to be designed to meet the unique demands of the situation and to identify and define clearly the issues considered, and allow adequate time to conduct the consultation.
4. Effective consultation requires openness about why people are consulted, how they will be consulted, and how much influence stakeholders will have in the policy decision.
5. Communication is essential to consultation. Those consulted need to be provided with comprehensive, balanced and accurate information.
6. All interested parties should have access to the consultation process.
7. All participants should be treated with dignity and respect.

Office of the Cabinet, 1993:30

agenda of such meetings should be clear in advance, as well as the kind of information that will be useful

- reaching an 'unorganised' public is more difficult, and may rely on circulating written proposals, calling public meetings, using talk-back radio and other techniques designed to solicit opinions
- agencies must avoid 'consultation overload', particularly with voluntary community groups, by coordinating processes, stakeholders and schedules among departments
- enough time is needed for representative bodies to consult their members. For most consultations, three months should be the norm and two months the absolute minimum
- consultation places a burden on those consulted. To minimise these costs, any written information should be concise and show clearly the issues at stake.

## When consultation is complete

- comments should be acknowledged as soon as possible
- it is important to 'close the loop'. Interest groups and the public should know how their input has been used. This is essential for building trust and credibility for future consultative processes
- details of the outcome should be provided to commentators. Feedback should include a summary of the views and information collected, and the resulting proposals or action
- processes for listening to citizens after policies are implemented can help identify problems on a continuing basis, and ensure continuous improvement.

## Consultation traps

- not all citizen action groups or industry spokespersons are legitimate representatives of their community. The basis on which people claim to speak for others must be clear
- highly organised and expert interest groups are most likely to participate in the process, digest the information offered and provide substantive comments

> Community-based consultations require elaborate and careful planning in order to reach a wide audience in a meaningful way. Opinion polls are a reliable guide to what the public already knows, but fail to measure the potential for change. Focus groups, citizens' panels and other local consultations require higher levels of commitment from government, and may reveal an unwelcome range of views. Bureaucracies typically lack the expertise to run such consultations effectively, and must often be re-organised in advance of any such initiative in order to become competent and open to their benefits. When properly organised, such approaches offer the prospect of far better policy, particularly in regard to implementation issues and emerging problems in the policy system.
> Mark Considine, 1994:162

**Table 7.2** Canada's principles of consultation

1. Consultation with Canadians is intrinsic to effective public policy development and service to the public. It should be the first thought, not an after-thought.
2. To be effective, consultation must be based on openness, trust, integrity, mutual respect for the legitimacy and point of view of all participants.
3. The outcome of consultation should not be predetermined. Consultation should not be used to communicate decisions already taken.
4. The initiative to consult may come from inside government or outside — each should respond as constructively as it can.
5. Whenever possible, consultation should involve all parties who can contribute to or are affected by the outcome of legislation.
6. Participants in consultation should have clear mandates. Participants should have influence over the outcome and a stake in implementing any action agreed upon.
7. Some participants may not have the resources or expertise required to participate. Thus, financial assistance or other support may be needed for their representation to be assured.
8. Effective consultation is about partnership. It implies shared responsibility and commitment: a clear, mutual understanding of the issues, objectives, purpose, and expectations of all parties is essential; the agenda and process should be negotiable; any constraints should be considered from the outset.
9. Participants should have a realistic idea of how much time a consultation is likely to take and plan for this in designing a process.
10. All participants must have timely access to relevant and easily understandable information and commit themselves to sharing information.
11. Effective consultation will not always lead to agreement; however, it should lead to a better understanding of each other's positions.
12. Where consultation does lead to agreement, whenever possible, participants should hold themselves accountable for implementing the resulting recommendations.
13. Effective consultation requires follow-through. Participants are entitled to know what use is made of the views and information they provide; they should also be made aware of the impact their ideas and involvement ultimately have on government decision making.
14. The skills required for effective communication are: listening, communicating, negotiating and consensus building. Participants should be trained in these skills.

Taken from 'Consultation Guidelines for Managers in the Federal Public Service', Privy Council Office, Canada, 1992, cited in OECD, 1994:12–13.

- there is a risk professional lobby groups will dominate consultation processes, particularly if the issues are technical, complex or otherwise difficult to communicate for less organised or financed groups.

## Consultation

Consultation is essential but often not easy. It can be difficult to identify all the stakeholders in a policy area. Often there are multiple interests at stake — those who will benefit from a new toll road, but also people living in the path of the development, businesses along the old road that will lose custom, environmental concerns about a forest or area of cultural significance along the way, lobbies for and against greater access to the new transport corridor. Each will criticise the process if they do not achieve their desired result.

Without consultation, legitimate and workable solutions to many problems prove elusive. Rather than despair at the complications, policy makers must develop better tools for consultation, providing opportunities for greater participation in the policy cycle.

# Chapter 8
# Coordination

Policies should be based on shared goals. Programs should work together, and not at cross-purposes. Priorities must be assigned between competing proposals. Coordination in government is a virtue.

Government consistency is about —
- internal congruity of policies and decisions
- equal treatment of citizens or regions within the jurisdiction
- appropriate behaviour by officials
- adherence to due process and official procedures
- projecting a public image showing that government knows what it is doing and what it wants (Wanna et al., 1993:1/14).

Achieving consistency by coordinating within government is not easy. The complexity and scale of government, and the need for specialisation, make it impossible for any one person — or even a committee such as cabinet — to keep all the relevant variables in play. The considerable cost of perfectly meshing policies and programs can outweigh the benefits. Coordination may be necessary, but it is an ideal realised only with many compromises. Governments have multiple and sometimes conflicting goals. Decision makers and policy advisers must learn to live with some incoherence. Coordination at least aims to minimise harmful inconsistencies.

Governments include a coordination phase in their policy cycle because they seek tolerable compatibility across activities. They institutionalise coordination through a combination of procedures — routines imposed on players in the policy process — and structures, in particular those organisations within government charged with a coordinating role.

**Snapshot**

Governments strive to work in a coordinated way, so the parts pull together.

They institutionalise coordination through routines and structures. Routines are procedures required of policy advisers. Structures include those central agencies that manage the routines and provide whole of government advice to key ministers.

This chapter describes the routines and structures used in Australian governments, and the relationship between bureaucratic coordination and political control.

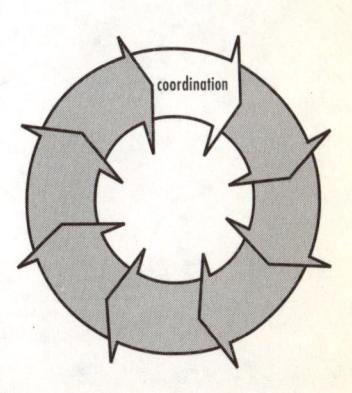

> Due process is ... an important safeguard against overloading decision makers. The processes involved in getting issues to the cabinet table are designed to assist cabinet to focus on broad strategic matters rather than petty detail. As far as possible details and questions of fact are settled outside cabinet by ministers and their advisers and, if necessary, by the appropriate cabinet committee.
>
> Michael Keating, 1996:64.

A first step is requiring agencies to consult within government, since this allows other departments to offer suggestions about the appropriateness of a new policy proposal and draws the proposal into the framework of existing programs administered by those other agencies.

Review by central agencies follows. This imposes a 'whole of government' perspective, in which a particular policy idea from a line department is compared with the overall policy direction of government.

Central agencies ask a number of simple questions — usually imposed by the format of cabinet submissions — about the policy, financial and administrative implications of a proposal. Is the submission consistent with existing objectives? Can it be afforded? Are there legal or organisational issues? Are there consequences for particular interest groups? Who was consulted and what was their response?

The answers — those supplied by line departments and those reached by central agencies — form the basis of policy briefs to senior ministers. Such briefs are the instrument of coordination. They let cabinet decide about consistency.

## An overall policy framework

Modern governments are networks of loosely linked organisations rather than a single hierarchy amenable to command and control (Painter, 1987:9). Departments and statutory authorities have their own goals and perspectives. Coordination amid this complexity requires rules about giving advice to decision makers. The policy process must include ways for advisers to —

- acknowledge potential conflict over policy goals
- consider the arguments in a structured way
- arrive at a recommendation.

Ideally a government will have a well developed and widely distributed policy framework, setting out economic, social and environmental objectives. It will behave corporately, a unity with multiple parts in pursuit of the same goals.

In practice, such overall policy frameworks are rarely documented cohesively. Policy goals are usually scattered through many sources — budget papers, major statements such as white papers, electoral pronouncements, social justice strategies and recent legislation. Occasionally a prime minister or premier makes a landmark speech outlining a comprehensive program. More often, overall policy objectives must be inferred from various sources and tested through consultation and coordination.

Central agencies work to key ministers, in particular the prime minister and treasurer, who are key players in establishing this overall framework. Like line departments, central agencies often work from clues rather than explicit statements of intent. But proximity to decision makers and consistent involvement in policy development across government ensure central agencies are well informed about government pronouncements and intentions. Hence central agencies act both as a resource for departments about policy frameworks, and advise cabinet on the fit between a proposal and the heritage of policy choices.

## Coordination routines

Central agencies use standardised routines to gather the information needed to test the consistency of a submission with other government objectives. Routines require agencies to state, for example, whether funding is available, or the social, economic or environmental implications of the proposal. Central agencies coordinate intergovernmental discussions through mechanisms such as the Council of Australian Governments (COAG), or one of the many ministerial coordinating committees that bring representatives of the Commonwealth, states, territories and sometimes local government into policy forums.

The routines of coordination are little more than a checklist of questions asked by central agencies about policy proposals. These query the importance of an issue, the quality of the original policy analysis, the choice of instruments, the depth of consultation. If the submission lacks information or does not answer serious concerns about the proposal, central agencies request more detail from the originating department. The objective is not to obstruct policy ideas (despite occasional appearances and robust complaints from line agencies and even ministers) but to ensure submissions address all relevant aspects of the proposal, and thus empower cabinet to make well-informed decisions.

Coordination is pursued through procedure, starting with the very format of the cabinet submission, demanding detail against a range of headings. The draft submission is circulated to relevant agencies for consultation comments, and then lodged with the central agencies, which check

> Central agencies have the particular responsibility of bringing a whole of government perspective to policy advising and advising on the overall coherence of policy. Their contribution is most often found in those areas where the interactive effects of individual policies cross portfolio boundaries. This is, of course, typical of the issues which need cabinet attention. In addition, central agencies may become involved if the issues have significant implications for the government's overall strategy.
> Michael Keating, 1996:64

> Power which flows from the practices of governing depends on the mundane but orderly world of routines, those repetitions which institutionalise behaviour. Routines give purpose to actions, making them part of a wider process. By habitualising us to play a role, routines provide predictability within an organisation, and the possibility of coordinating a wider enterprise. They link individuals to process and values, and so make coordination possible. Through routines which turn rules into habits, the centre can act at a distance.
> Glyn Davis, 1995:135

information, evaluate content and often suggest modifications. Only then does the submission proceed to cabinet for its decision.

In their briefing papers to ministers, central agencies offer a whole of government perspective asking policy, financial and administrative questions about a cabinet submission. Ministers and their advisers add the political dimension.

From a policy perspective, central agencies check that proposals —

- are logical and well considered
- are consistent with other government announcements
- are consistent with governing party policy
- are consistent with intergovernmental and international obligations
- meet cabinet guidelines
- have no presentational problems, and
- are suitably timed.

From a financial perspective, central agencies must ensure —

- money is really needed
- the initiative is cost-effective
- the right priorities are met
- the overall budget is not exceeded, and
- there are no hidden traps likely to require sudden funding increases.

Finally, from an administrative perspective, central agencies will report on any implications of a policy proposal for —

- public sector employment
- employment or industrial relations
- equity and fairness considerations.

The division of responsibility for examining these issues varies across jurisdictions. Generally, however, policy issues are pursued by the central policy agency (e.g. PM&C), financial questions by Treasury and personnel arrangements by the management agency (see Wanna et al., 1993:1/15–16). The prime minister will receive briefs from all three, along with political advice from the prime minister's office. One important job of the leader is to maintain the general strategy of the government. These briefs from central

> Coordination is one of the golden words of our time. I cannot offhand think of any way in which the word is used that implies disapproval. Policies should be coordinated; they should not run every which-way. No one wishes their children to be described as uncoordinated. Many of the world's ills are attributed to lack of coordination in government ... Policies should be mutually supportive rather than contradictory. People should not work at cross purposes. The participants in any particular activity should contribute to a common purpose at the right time and in the right amount to achieve coordination. A should facilitate B in order to achieve C.
>
> Aaron Wildavsky, 1973:142

agencies are therefore an important coordination mechanism, a way to pull together the diverse threads of policy.

## Central agencies

Government is divided into departments, each with its own mission, culture and resources. Departmentalisation allows specialisation and focus, but it risks dividing government into contradictory programs, with pointless competition between units and inconsistent outcomes for citizens.

Central agencies work to resist this fragmentation by providing consistent rules and processes. They view government as a single undertaking that needs balance among devolved responsibilities and adherence to a shared set of norms.

The managerialist ethos of the 1980s and 1990s has been critical of rigid rules imposed by the centre, particularly in financial and workforce management issues. But even governments committed to a managerialist approach insist on a role for central agencies in assessing policy proposals. A 'whole of government' perspective from the centre allows ministers, especially leaders, to impose consistency on the vast array of decisions before any cabinet.

The list of 'central agencies' is flexible, varying between jurisdictions, and changing over time and by issue. Because all governments must address policy, financial, legal and administrative issues, agencies tend to be organised around these responsibilities.

*Central policy agency*

In Canberra, central policy coordination is the responsibility the Department of Prime Minister and Cabinet. In the states and territories, this task falls to the cabinet office or the department of premier and cabinet or chief minister. Some large local government authorities have developed a similar central policy capacity around the office of the mayor.

The PM&C (1997) accepts a 'particular responsibility for policy coordination'. The department must ensure 'the prime minister has the best possible advice drawing from, and consulting with, appropriate sources across the whole of the government system'.

More broadly, PM&C's role is to —
- ensure policy proposals put to the prime minister, other

---

The Department of Prime Minister and Cabinet in Canberra divides policy officers across divisions which mirror activity within government —
- Aboriginal Reconciliation Branch
- Economic Division
- Industries, Resources and Environment Division
- Social Policy Division
- International Division
- Commonwealth–State Relations Secretariat
- Cabinet Secretariat
- Parliament and Government Division
- Office of the Status of Women
- Office of Indigenous Affairs
- Corporate Services Division

Department of the Prime Minister and Cabinet, 1997

---

The Ministry of Premier and Cabinet in Western Australia has as its corporate mission 'To ensure the premier's requirements and those of cabinet are met.'

> In Victoria, the functions of the Cabinet Office are —
> - to assist the premier as chair of cabinet in leadership of the government, management of the cabinet agenda and coordination of government policy development and implementation
> - to provide policy analysis and advice to the premier on all matters affecting his role as head of government and to provide administrative support for the operation of the cabinet, cabinet committees and executive council and for the government's relationship with the parliament
> - to assist the premier in identifying emerging issues, carrying out practical forward planning, reviewing policy and assessing the impact of government decisions and actions, and
> - on behalf of the premier, to lead and participate in policy development and coordination action to reform and revitalise the government of Victoria and the Victorian economy.
>
> Department of Premier and Cabinet, 1996

ministers in the portfolio and to cabinet are developed in a coherent, informed and coordinated fashion
- where directed, to coordinate the administrative response to government policies and decisions, recognising that ministers are responsible individually for the administration of their departments and collectively for matters decided by cabinet, and
- to provide services to the prime minister and to the government to enable the business of government to be managed in an efficient, effective and coordinated manner.

These objectives, shared by Commonwealth and state central policy agencies, require an agency structure that mirrors activities across government. The central policy agency needs experts in every major area facing government, to test views offered by line departments. These policy officers, often drawn from the agencies they monitor, are the core staff of policy coordination.

In Victoria, for example, as shown in Table 8.1, branches within the Cabinet Office are explicitly designed to observe policy activities in particular agencies.

This structure allows the Cabinet Office to provide advice to the premier on every matter before government. It also provides a capacity to coordinate intergovernmental negotiations. The relevant branch will work closely with line agencies to ensure a consistent state position on various working parties, and to ensure the premier is briefed fully before attending government leaders' meetings.

Central policy agencies in other jurisdictions operate in similar ways. Indeed, senior officials from Canberra, the states and territories now meet regularly, or converse on national telephone links to provide a measure of consistency in policy advice across borders.

Briefs prepared by the central policy agency are forwarded to the prime minister, premier or chief minister. There will be a brief on every item before cabinet, regular 'topical' briefs on matters of the day, and occasionally longer briefs that explore emerging or long-running issues.

Leaders thus chair cabinet armed with an array of information and analysis supplied by central agencies. They can question ministers on details of a proposal, or how it fits into the wider scheme of government.

**Table 8.1** Victorian Cabinet Office branches and their responsibilities

| Cabinet office branch | Client agency/department |
|---|---|
| Social Policy | Health and Community Services, Justice, Education |
| Resources and Infrastructure | Conservation and Natural Resources, Agriculture, Energy and Minerals, Planning and Development, Transport |
| Economic Development | Treasury and Finance, Business and Employment, Arts, Sport and Tourism |
| Government | Treasury and Finance (Budget and Finance) |
| Intergovernmental Relations & Strategic Planning | Treasury and Finance |
| Legal and Secretariat | Across government and cabinet |

*Treasury*

As the central policy agency advises on policy activity, so central financial agencies keep a close eye on the fiscal implications of existing and proposed policies. This function typically sits in the 'budget' division of the state treasury or Commonwealth Department of Finance.

When a line department prepares a cabinet submission, it must consult with the central financial agency. Finance will certify that the costings on the proposal are 'agreed' — that is, the figures included in the submission accurately reflect the likely costs of the proposed program. Such agreement does not mean the treasurer will support the proposal in cabinet, nor that the department will brief its minister supportively, only that the sums are accurate.

Central financial agencies manage the annual budget cycle that sets priorities among all programs for the year ahead. Line departments make bids for new policy funds, through their minister, as part of the budget round. The central financial agency is likely to oppose spending outside the budget process, since this upsets fiscal forecasts and undermines budget discipline.

> The Commonwealth Department of Finance includes among its functions —
> - advice on appropriate overall budgetary and financial policy issues
> - information, advice and systems to enable government to translate broad priorities into detailed programs in the annual budget process
> - analysis and evaluation of new spending proposals and review of existing programs
> - advising on techniques to evaluate the impact of expenditure programs and proposals
> - accounting services to government departments and budget dependent agencies
> - fostering efficient and effective human resource management and financial practices in departments, statutory authorities and government business enterprises
> - advice on occupational superannuation schemes for Commonwealth employees and parliamentarians
> - major service wide production systems for payroll processing and financial management, and
> - conduct of major asset sales as required.

Cabinet submissions put forward outside the budget cycle therefore focus on implementation of policy proposals included in the budget papers. Nonetheless, governments must respond to issues not anticipated in the budget, and maintain reserves (known in some jurisdictions as 'the Treasurer's Reserve') to deal with these contingencies. Alternatively, agencies with an urgent policy proposal are instructed to find the necessary funds within their existing allocation.

The treasury or finance department is likely to provide a brief for its minister on most matters in the cabinet agenda, just as central policy agencies brief the chair of cabinet. The advice will be concerned principally, but not exclusively, with financial considerations. The brief is forwarded to the treasurer, with a summary of any concerns from other departments incorporated into the leader's briefing papers.

Like cabinet offices, budget divisions tend to mirror the structures of government. Budget officers become expert in the portfolios they monitor, working closely with line agencies on new proposals. The Commonwealth Department of Finance, for example, views the 'analysis and evaluation of new spending proposals' as one of its central tasks. A prudent department will discuss a policy proposal with Finance before presenting a cabinet submission.

### Attorney-General's Department

When submissions carry legal implications, or require new legislation, line departments must consult with the government's legal agencies. Depending on the matter at hand, consultation may be required with the Attorney-General's Department, the Crown or Solicitor-General and the Parliamentary Counsel.

It is embarrassing (and often expensive) for governments to make mistakes in legal issues, and so great care is taken to ensure appropriate scrutiny before cabinet is asked to make a decision. The Commonwealth *Cabinet Handbook* (PM&C, 1994:25), for example, sets down very strict requirements about consultation for submissions with legal requirements. It suggests legislation be considered only as a 'last resort'. The Attorney-General's Department is required to certify that the proposed legislation is necessary; not even a draft submission can be circulated for consultation 'until cleared by the Attorney-General's Department'.

*Central personnel agencies*

When a submission has implications for the public sector workforce, advice is sometimes sought from the agency with responsibility for personnel. In most jurisdictions this function is attached to the Premier's Department, though some states and the Commonwealth retain free standing personnel agencies, such as Canberra's Public Service and Merit Protection Commission.

Such advice may be included in the brief provided by the central policy agency, or forwarded directly to the responsible minister. In the Commonwealth, for example, the minister assisting the prime minister for public service matters may take to the cabinet table a brief on any public sector consequences from a submission.

Employment implications may also attract the interest of departments responsible for employment or industrial relations. However, increasingly employees are treated as an element of budget rather than managed separately, and detailed personnel implications are left for the relevant line department to settle.

*Other consultation*

A line agency with a policy proposal to put before cabinet must consult all the central line agencies, which must be persuaded a proposal makes sense from a whole of government perspective, and has been cleared for financial and legal consequences, with proper consideration of public sector implications. This is often a process of bargaining, with significant modification of a submission before it finally reaches the cabinet agenda.

The coordination process does not stop with the central agencies. The Commonwealth *Cabinet Handbook* (PM&C, 1994:21–23) lists a daunting array of Commonwealth agencies to be consulted if affected by proposals. These can include —

- Aboriginal and Torres Strait Islander Commission for policy matters with implications for indigenous Australians
- Department of Employment, Education, Training and Youth Affairs for policy proposals which might affect young people
- Department of Prime Minister and Cabinet for issues influencing women or multicultural concerns

---

The Public Service and Merit Protection Commission in Canberra sets out its mission and role in the following terms —

*Our Corporate Mission*

We promote, support and model excellence in people management so as to provide the best possible public service for the government and the people of Australia.

*Our Role*

We see our role as —

- articulating and defending the ethos of public service
- contributing to the collective leadership of the public service
- working in partnership with the public sector agencies
- providing external review of public sector decisions
- facilitating continuous improvement, and
- acting as a repository of best practice in people management.

*Our Corporate Goals*

We seek to achieve an efficient, effective and accountable public service which —

- applies merit, fairness, and equity
- demonstrates a high standard of professional and ethical behaviour
- develops and maintains high quality leadership
- promotes best practice in people management, and
- recognises and develops the diverse skills of all its people.

Public Service and Merit Protection Commission, 1996

- Productivity Commission for regulatory matters
- Treasury and Australian Taxation Office for taxation issues
- Department of Environment, Sports and Territories for proposals with environmental consequences
- Department of Foreign Affairs and Trade or Australian Agency for International Development (AusAID) for issues concerning assistance to other countries.

The list can be expanded endlessly at Commonwealth level and for each state and territory. This consultation is intended to assist coordination. It brings the proposals of one agency into alignment with practices elsewhere in government. Since agency boundaries overlap, prior discussions about policy proposals settle disputes and lock in support before cabinet deliberation.

### Coordination comments

Cabinet practice varies across jurisdictions, but in all Australian governments cabinet submissions must include detail of consultation with other government agencies. This introduces contestability into the policy process.

These 'coordination comments' advise ministers on views about a policy proposal from within and beyond government. They alert cabinet to any inconsistencies between the proposals in the submission and practices elsewhere in government.

As the Commonwealth *Cabinet Handbook* (PM&C, 1994:23) states —

> Consultation is an integral part of the development of a policy proposal, from the outset of that development through to clearance of a final draft submission. Ministers and officers in departments with an interest should have ample opportunity to contribute to the development of the proposal and to resolve any differences before lodgement of the submission.

The *Cabinet Handbook* stresses that agencies must take on board coordination comments, either dealing with the objection or modifying recommendations accordingly. Should they fail to so do, 'Cabinet Office may reject a submission (unless there are excellent mitigating reasons)

---

> When one bureaucrat tells another to coordinate a policy, he means that it should be cleared with other official participants who have some stake in the matter. This is a way of sharing the blame in case things go wrong (each initial on the documents being another hostage against retribution). Since they cannot be coerced, their consent must be obtained. Bargaining must take place to reconcile the differences with the result that the policy may be modified, even at the cost of compromising its original purposes. Coordination in this sense is another word for consent.
>
> Aaron Wildavsky, 1973:143

where strong criticism by other departments has not been addressed in the submission or where significant issues have been canvassed' (PM&C, 1994:31)

Commonwealth cabinet procedures require that in cases of disagreement, dissenting coordination comments be 'included in full as the final attachment to the submission' (PM&C, 1994:30). Ministers can thus read the views of interested parties when considering a submission.

Coordination comments allow cabinet to compare a particular policy proposal with the overall framework of government direction.

### Coordination in departments

Every complex organisation must grapple with ways to bring its disparate parts together. This is as true of individual departments as it is for governments, though on a smaller scale. The policy domain within agencies is usually charged by the chief executive with orderly management of policy processes and documents, with fulfilling the centre's demands for routine and extensive intra-governmental consultation, and with testing the integrity and quality of divisional proposals.

Thus one finds policy divisions and liaison units within departments, close to the secretary or director-general, responsible for internal coordination, liaison with the centre, and smooth management of inter agency and ministerial council negotiations. Finance divisions or economists in policy units may scrutinise costings; the advice of personnel sections may be required on human resource implications, mirroring their counterparts in the centre of government.

Like central agencies, departmental policy groups develop keen sensitivity to policy shifts, an ability to predict responses from within and without, and astuteness about the demands of the political and policy domains.

Like central agencies, departmental policy specialists experience tensions as they strive to coordinate within, to find common ground and to arm the ministers properly for cabinet's deliberations.

### Coordination and politics

Some issues cannot be resolved through consultation or central agency coordination. When disagreement centres on

> Politics is not the art of the possible. It consists in choosing between the disastrous and the unpalatable.
>
> John Kenneth Galbraith

politics rather than policy, central agencies can only present the facts and leave the argument to be settled by ministers.

Many policy arguments reflect the clashing agendas of departments. A proposal to increase woodchip exports might attract support from the Department of Primary Industries but strong opposition from Environment. Consultation will highlight differences in opinion rather than create consensus. The central agency brief can point to the strengths and weaknesses of the proposal, to national and international agreements, to scientific evidence and expert opinion. They may sometimes propose one or more compromise recommendations. Yet only cabinet can make the final, difficult choice.

In some cases, governments decide to live with inconsistency. For decades, state governments funded public health campaigns against smoking yet subsidised tobacco farmers. Governments have many clients, often with incompatible demands. Coordination is essential, but in the end, politics rules.

*Coordination*

Coordination routines seek consistency in government. They require line agencies to consult other affected departments. Submissions must then be discussed with the central agencies, which look to the policy, financial and administrative implications from a whole of government perspective. Those central agencies brief their ministers on the compatibility of a new policy proposal with the existing policy framework.

Coordination systems inevitably create tension between line agencies and those at the centre. For line departments, coordination routines can seem frustrating impediments, causing delay and adding to the reporting burden. Ministers, unused to questioning, may bristle. Such tension is unavoidable. The desire for whole of government consistency means little to a line manager, struggling to deliver a program with stretched resources, yet required to seek cabinet approval for some modification or staff appointment. In any coordination process the costs are felt by those in the field, while the gains belong to the centre.

This imbalance places a special responsibility on those in central agencies to use their authority lightly, to avoid unnecessary demands on line departments, and to explain the wider purpose behind their request for information or

> My experience in government is that when things are non-controversial and beautifully coordinated, there is not much going on ...
> John F. Kennedy

further work on a submission. Central agency arrogance is inappropriate and unhelpful. Government looks very different from a line department than from the centre, because people are pursuing very different purposes. Central agencies matter because they help government to operate as a single unit. But unless line departments are allowed to get on with the tangible business of government — delivering services — coordination is a pointless paper exercise.

# Chapter 9
# The Decision

**Snapshot**

Finally, it is time for a decision. This is the pivotal point, when the analyst's work is judged by cabinet. Yet this step in the policy cycle is also regulated and made routine.

Who makes the decision? What material is before them? How are decisions recorded? This chapter explores the routine of cabinet deliberations.

Cabinet's decision is the pivot of the public policy cycle, the point on which all previous and subsequent work turns. Here, political judgement is delivered in light of all the technical advice, the options, the analysis, the comparison of possible instruments, the consultation and the coordination efforts.

From the universe of issues and problems, a small number have been selected, developed and stated for cabinet's decision about the future.

At any time, many thousands of proposals are before government. They occupy different places in the policy cycle, some nearing completion, others barely formulated. Most are working towards this moment, when they find a place on the cabinet agenda.

Cabinet convenes each week to consider and decide on a dozen, or even fewer, submissions. A cabinet decision brings legitimacy and the prospect of implementation. If a submission passes over this all important hurdle, it is on the way to becoming public policy.

The sheer volume of material awaiting consideration, and the need for at least minimum standards of information and analysis, mean that cabinets must operate by strict rules. Submissions follow a predetermined format. They are considered in a set order. Decisions are recorded and distributed according to a standard process.

Cabinet is the only opportunity for ministers, acting collectively, to consider the full range of ideas before government. Much is at stake and time is always short. When discussing submissions, ministers must balance political consequences, policy objectives, administrative convenience, media attractiveness and their own place in history. Given this pressure, ministers insist on proper process, so that all necessary data and advice are before them when choosing.

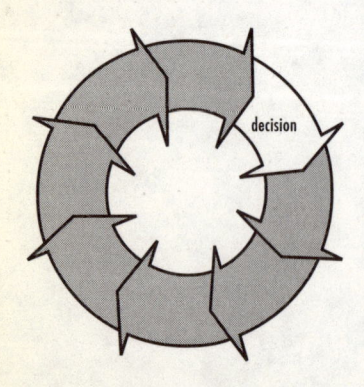

Policy advisers must be proficient thoroughly in the rules governing cabinet. A good policy idea is not enough, even if consultation and coordination indicate widespread support. Proposals must answer all the questions posed in the format for submissions. They must be supported with financial, legal and social impact data, and any other relevant information. Ministers want to make informed decisions. The routines of cabinet government are designed to ensure consistency, coherence and clarity, and to reinforce the political nature of this pivotal moment. Neglecting these routines diminishes the effectiveness of cabinet.

## Cabinet routines

Cabinet routines are expressed as rules, and usually codified in a cabinet handbook (see, for example, PM&C, 1994). These set out formats for all types of submission, and timelines for consideration.

Cabinet routines establish a timetable for business within government. Because cabinet meets weekly, agencies can organise their work agenda around the cabinet schedule. Cabinet also requires certain regular submissions — quarterly performance indicators, budget submissions, annual strategic plans and reports. Government is always prone to crisis and disruption, but the orderly business of cabinet provides some measure of stability and predictability.

The policy cycle has been in play long before cabinet considers a submission. Once an issue has been identified, a line department undertakes policy analysis and makes recommendations to the minister about an appropriate policy instrument. The ministerial office may offer views. The minister must approve further policy development. A discussion paper or draft submission may be circulated and feedback sought from related government agencies and key interest groups. Following consultation, the draft submission, by now well developed, is forwarded to the central agencies for consideration and comment. Only with the consultation and coordination phases complete is an agency finally ready to approach cabinet through its minister for a decision.

The Commonwealth cabinet process provides a reasonably standard Australian model for cabinet deliberations, though routines vary slightly across jurisdictions —

- once cleared by the central policy agency, a submission

---

**A checklist for good cabinet submissions**

Ask yourself —

- is the submission necessary?
- should it be a submission seeking a decision or, alternatively, an information paper?
- are the objectives of the submission clear?
- does the submission achieve the objectives it sets for itself?
- does the submission include all reasonable options and no unrealistic options?
- has the necessary level of consultation inside and outside government taken place? Does it indicate whether the views of the major affected groups are known?
- are winners and losers clearly identified?
- are precedent considerations addressed?
- has consistency with arrangements/directions in other jurisdictions been addressed?
- are financial implications clear and proposals properly costed (in conjunction with treasury)?
- are recommendations clear and uncomplicated? Do they flow from the body of the submission?
- is the submission drafted clearly and is it well structured?

Source: John Wanna et al., 1994:2/27.

> **Cabinet**
>
> While not mentioned in the constitution, cabinet is the central organ for collective consideration of issues by ministers. Although the recorded outcomes of cabinet discussions are often referred to as decisions, the holder of legal authority to make the decision is often the executive council, an individual minister or an official with specific statutory powers.
>
> John Howard, 1996:1

is lodged with the cabinet office at least 10 days before cabinet consideration

- the submission must follow the standard format required in the *Cabinet Handbook*, with details of prior consultation and warning of any likely complications or objections
- a submission is divided into three parts — a *cover sheet* summarising key points, a *body* spelling out the proposal, and any *attachments* with supporting data. Commonwealth cabinet rules restrict the combined cover sheet and body to just six pages
- a cabinet 'folder' or 'bag' (actually one or more envelopes of documents) is circulated late in the week before the cabinet meeting to allow scrutiny by ministers and their advisers. Cabinets typically meet early in the week. The Commonwealth cabinet, for example, meets on Mondays in parliamentary sitting weeks and on Tuesdays in non-sitting weeks
- submissions at the cabinet meeting are considered according to an agenda prepared by the cabinet secretary and approved by the prime minister as chair of cabinet
- the minister presenting a submission puts the case for cabinet acceptance, and debate may follow. At the close of discussion, the chair may sum up, perhaps suggesting words for the decision to reflect the meeting's mood. Votes in cabinet are rare; a submission with insufficient support in the room tends to lapse, or be deferred for further development
- after the meeting, the cabinet secretary draws up the minutes and, if necessary, confirms these with the prime minister. Decisions (sometimes known as cabinet minutes) are then circulated to agencies for action or information.

Cabinet is not discussed in the Commonwealth constitution. Even the secrecy of cabinet meetings has been successfully challenged, with recent court judgments opening for scrutiny the notebooks used by the cabinet note takers.

Yet there is no question cabinet retains a central role in the Australian system of government. The executive controls the numbers in parliament, so cabinet decisions are legitimate and authoritative. Cabinet sets the agenda for the executive and the public service. Cabinet is the forum in which choices are endorsed, information exchanged, initiatives coordinated, strategy endorsed and decisions made.

> The cabinet plays a key role in bringing together and in reconciling different viewpoints, but it requires an orderly process to do this.
>
> Michael Keating, 1996:63

**Table 9.1** Cabinet conventions and procedures

| | |
|---|---|
| collective responsibility | Cabinet ministers must publicly support all decisions taken in cabinet, whatever view they advanced during the meeting. A cabinet minister who cannot accept collective responsibility should resign |
| ministerial responsibility | Ministers are responsible for the submissions they bring forward, even though others may have developed and drafted the material |
| portfolios | Ministers represent their portfolios in cabinet. Public servants or advisers cannot deputise for a minister in cabinet |
| policy approval | Major policy initiatives cannot be announced or implemented until approved by cabinet (unless cleared by the prime minister) |
| confidentiality | To reach the best decisions, cabinet discussions must be frank. The meeting, together with all related documents, subject to strict confidentiality |
| interests | In cabinet discussions, ministers must indicate any conflict of interest concerning a submission, and excuse themselves from deliberations if appropriate |
| committees | The decisions of cabinet committees are not binding until endorsed by cabinet |
| agenda | The agenda is usually approved in advance by the chair of cabinet, along with the contents of the cabinet folders |
| non-agenda items | An item not listed for discussion can be raised only with the prior agreement of the chair of cabinet |
| 10 day rule | To ensure sufficient time for evaluation and briefing of ministers, submissions must be lodged 10 days before cabinet meets |
| circulation | Several days before each cabinet meeting the cabinet secretariat will circulate folders containing submissions, memoranda and other cabinet material. These are subject to secrecy provisions, and cannot be shown to others outside cabinet security protocols |
| submissions | Cabinet submissions must include all information specified in the *Cabinet Handbook*, be of no more than six pages (excluding attachments), signed and, if concerned with policy, contain options and recommendations |
| secrecy | All cabinet submissions must include a secrecy classification level and be marked 'cabinet-in-confidence' |
| secretary | The secretary of cabinet is bound by the same rules of secrecy as ministers, and must never breach the confidentiality of the cabinet process |
| note takers | The secretary may be supported by note takers, who are also bound by cabinet confidentiality. While notebooks may include comments that assist in framing decisions, no verbatim record is made of the meeting |
| officials | Officials other than note takers attend meetings only with the permission of the chair of cabinet, and only to answer questions about factual or technical matters. Officials should leave the room before any decision is taken |
| decisions | In theory the chair approves the wording of decisions before circulation. In practice officials write up cabinet minutes. Ministers can object to the wording at the next meeting or in writing to the prime minister |
| records | The records created by a government are only available to that government. New governments do not have access to the cabinet records of their predecessors |

> Submissions are papers containing recommendations by the responsible minister(s) on action to be taken by the government.
>
> John Howard, 1996:5

Within the policy cycle, cabinet's decision settles disagreement. A submission may have strong supporters and detractors within government. Only cabinet can consider and finalise the issue. Cabinet consideration is the one moment in the policy cycle when all perspectives focus on a single proposal, and the arguments translate to a decision.

## What goes to cabinet?

Cabinet ministers sometimes complain of being overloaded, of having to read and think about too many different policy problems. Agencies, on the other hand, may be frustrated by an inability to get urgent business on to the cabinet agenda.

Establishing firm rules about what cabinet will consider is a difficult task. Ministers need sufficient information to feel in control, yet they also wish to maintain a strategic outlook, setting policy direction rather than trading in detail.

The Commonwealth *Cabinet Handbook* (PM&C, 1994:17–18) sets out guidelines for agencies about what matters should be considered by cabinet.

Some matters, though, must go to cabinet. In the Commonwealth these include —

- new policy proposals and proposed significant variations to existing policies
- proposals likely to have a significant effect on employment in either the public or private sector
- expenditure proposals, including proposals for major capital works and computer acquisitions (normally considered only in the budget context)
- proposals requiring legislation, other than minor proposals which the prime minister has agreed need not be raised in cabinet
- proposals likely to have a significant impact upon relations between the Commonwealth and foreign, state, territory or local governments
- proposed responses to recommendations made in parliamentary committee reports, except for responses which the prime minister agrees raise no significant policy questions
- government negotiation of, or agreement to, international treaties.

Similar statements govern cabinet procedures in most states and territories. All emphasise reducing the volume of

> A cabinet meeting might follow the standard format published by the Queensland government in its *Cabinet Handbook* —
> - apologies
> - confirmation of collective minutes from the previous meeting
> - policy submissions and memoranda
> - cabinet committee reports
> - legislative submissions
> - significant appointments proposals
> - information papers
> - matters without submission
> - minutes for executive council
> - ministers to attend executive council
> - invitations unable to be attended by the premier.
>
> Office of the Cabinet, 1995:23

business. Where agencies can settle a matter between them, or when a concern is not of sufficient importance to make a demand on cabinet's time, it must be resolved at a ministerial level. As the Commonwealth *Cabinet Handbook* (PM&C, 1994:17) notes, 'ministers should consider seriously the option of settling a matter by correspondence, particularly where it is likely that all interested ministers are in agreement'. If need be, the proposed solution can be then forwarded to the prime minister for approval.

As a matter of principle, cabinet declines to consider matters not listed on the agenda. The cabinet agenda shifts according to the interests of the chair and the issues before government.

In the Commonwealth, each type of submission has a specified format. *Policy submissions* are the most extensive, with 15 or more different headings which must be addressed. Policy submissions are signed by ministers and seek to commit the government to a course of action.

*Memoranda* are prepared and signed by departmental officials, usually in response to a cabinet request for further information or more options in some policy discussion.

*Committee reports* reflect the increasing importance of cabinet committees. Cabinet may have a series of standing and ad hoc committees to deal with the volume of business, and to provide focused discussion on sensitive or detailed issues (Howard, 1996:4). Almost all are nominally chaired by the prime minister, though in practice a senior minister may take the running. Many submissions pass through a committee before they get to cabinet, providing a forum for debate and negotiation among relevant ministers. If subsequent cabinet consideration is required, the committee recommendation is printed on blue paper, otherwise it is simply noted by cabinet. Ministers are reluctant to reopen in cabinet an issue already settled at committee level (Codd, 1990:6), and cannot do so if a member of that committee.

*Legislation submissions* take several forms, depending on the stage of the proposal —

- an *Authority to Prepare* submission invites cabinet to approve the broad outlines, and drafting instructions, for a new bill
- cabinet, or a cabinet legislation committee, may later consider an *Authority to Introduce* submission, which sets out the completed bill, outlines the consultation process and its results, and indicates how the proposed legislation differs from the outline originally approved.

> **Preparing submissions**
>
> Submissions and memoranda should —
>
> - be presented in a familiar format
> - be easy to 'navigate' around
> - put forward an agreed basis of facts on which discussion may proceed
> - succinctly identify the central issues
> - indicate realistic policy options and their implications for achieving identified objectives
>
> There are various techniques to achieve this —
>
> - use everyday language
> - avoid long, complicated sentences and paragraphs
> - avoid technical terms, jargon
> - be concise; stick to key points
> - build arguments step by step
> - rework each sentence until every word counts
> - edit ruthlessly
> - test the finished product by having it read by a colleague unfamiliar with the subject.
>
> PM&C, 1994:68

> Officials (other than cabinet officers) do not attend cabinet or committee meetings unless their attendance has been specifically requested by a minister and approved by the prime minister ...
>
> Officials are present only to aid their minister and, through him or her, to provide advice to the meeting if requested. They are expected to explain factual or technical matters on request, but not to participate in discussions. Officials normally leave the meeting before final outcomes are discussed.
>
> PM&C, 1994:14

> **Advice**
>
> Ministers will obtain advice from a range of sources, but primarily from their private office and from their departments. There is clearly no obligation on ministers to accept advice put to them by public servants, but it is important that advice be considered carefully and fairly. It is not for public servants to continue to press their advice beyond the point where their ministers have indicated that the advice, having been fully considered, is not the favoured approach. Public servants should feel free, however, to raise issues for reconsideration if they believe there are emerging problems or additional information that warrant fresh examination.
>
> John Howard, 1996:13

In some jurisdictions there are also separate submissions for *Significant Appointments*, though in the Commonwealth this is handled through a letter to the prime minister. In either case there is still a standard checklist covering the name and qualifications of the candidate, the nature of the office, regional and gender balance considerations, and any matters likely to cause controversy.

*Information Papers* inform cabinet of discussions in ministerial councils and the Council of Australian Governments (COAG). As inter-governmental relations become more complex, ministers need to know what options are being considered by their colleagues. Such items are described as 'under the line' because they are usually listed for noting rather than for discussion.

*Matters without Submission* are an opportunity to discuss urgent business. The prime minister may also address questions of political strategy or parliamentary business.

*Executive Council Minutes* are recommendations for appointments or expenditure required to be approved by the governor-general in council. In recent years these have been greatly reduced in number, and are not discussed by cabinet. Still, cabinet must ensure a schedule of ministers who will attend the formal meetings of the executive council. Cabinet may also allocate engagements for important events the prime minister is unable to attend, though this is typically handled through ministerial offices rather than in the cabinet room.

## Briefing ministers

Each type of submission carries a security classification. Only those advisers and public servants with appropriate security clearance can view a submission, and all governments have strict rules about the handling, distribution and filing of cabinet material.

Cabinet meetings last half a day or more, and can cover anything from national security to schedules of publicity appearances. Even ministers with no items on the agenda must be ready to discuss any proposals with cross-portfolio implications. Hence a key function of departments is to brief ministers on the contents of the cabinet folder. Ministers are not merely responsible for their portfolio: they are members of the executive council, and share responsibility for management of the entire policy agenda.

Each agency has its own format for briefings. Most keep a brief to a single page. The department will tell its minister what the submission is about, how it may affect the portfolio, indicate a position and possibly suggest amendments. The brief provides a script for the minister to participate in the debate, and a way for the agency to have its concerns heard in the cabinet room. Some briefs are the responsibility of the minister's office rather than the department.

For submissions prepared by the department, the brief will be more extensive. Ministers must be able to promote and defend their submissions. They need at their finger tips all the necessary facts and figures. Nervous ministers rehearse arguments with senior officials before going to cabinet. Later, senior line department managers cluster in the minister's office to learn whether cabinet accepted the departmental recommendations.

An important role for the prime minister in cabinet is to provide 'whole of government' scrutiny on submissions. As chair, the prime minister must stand above the interests of individual departments to consider the interests of the government. To assist in this, the prime minister is provided with extensive briefing notes on every agenda item. These include detailed analysis of the policy and financial consequences of a submission, and a recommendation for or against acceptance. These briefs are prepared by specialised policy officers from PM&C.

Many sources of advice make the prime minister the best informed participant in cabinet discussions, able to interrogate ministers about the detail and implications of their proposals.

The treasurer and the minister for finance also take extensive briefing notes to cabinet, though with an economic and budget emphasis. Other ministers with cross-government responsibilities, such as the attorney-general and the minister for industrial relations, may also work from specialised analysis of submissions. Any concerns held by their agencies, though, are also incorporated into briefs prepared by the Department of Prime Minister and Cabinet and by the Cabinet Policy Unit.

While departments provide ministers with technical advice, ministerial offices supply a political perspective on cabinet business. In particular, the prime minister's office advises on the electoral and media implications of submissions.

> The Cabinet Policy Unit, located in the Department of the Prime Minister and Cabinet, provides the prime minister with advice on issues before the cabinet and on the strategic policy directions of the government. The unit is staffed from within and outside the public service. The head of the Cabinet Policy Unit is the secretary to cabinet.
> John Howard, 1996:6

The Decision

> **Recommendations**
>
> Cabinet submissions must contain recommendations. These follow a standard format: 'I recommend that cabinet agree/approve/note …'
>
> A poorly crafted recommendation does not assist clear decision making —
>
> > I recommend that cabinet adopt proposals a) through e), as set out on page 5 of the submission.
>
> A good recommendation sets out clearly what action cabinet is being asked to take —
>
> > I recommend that cabinet approve an increase of 5,000 places in the family reunion immigration program for the coming financial year.
>
> The decision is then easy to state —
>
> > Cabinet decided to approve an increase of 5,000 places in the family reunion immigration program for the coming financial year.

These political judgements are prepared in a briefing note that, along with the department's advice, is presented to the prime minister in the cabinet folder above the submission in question.

The submissions and briefing notes draw together political, policy and administrative advice and bring them to the cabinet process. Ministers enter cabinet discussion alive to the implications of proposals. They have the information required to balance political interests with sound policy and to avoid unmanageable proposals. Cabinet becomes the central focus of government, the time and place when a political perspective engages with line departmental submissions to produce public policy choices.

## Recording cabinet decisions

The practice for recording cabinet decisions varies across jurisdictions. Some state governments ban all public servants from the cabinet room, relying on the premier or a seconded member of parliament to note decisions. Most jurisdictions, including the Commonwealth, prefer to support cabinet with a professional secretariat. These public servants prepare, collate and distribute cabinet papers, take notes during meetings, retrieve cabinet material for confidential storage, write up cabinet minutes, and distribute these to departments and ministers.

By tradition, elaborate procedures are used to code cabinet decisions. In Queensland, for example, different shades of paper indicate the significance of a decision. A record of decision on gold-edged paper is forwarded to the minister with implementation responsibility. Chief executives tasked by cabinet receive the relevant decision on silver-edged paper. For the rest, decisions arrive on blue paper — an interest in the decision but no implementation responsibility — or white for information only (Office of the Cabinet, 1995:24).

> The recommendations of a submission summarise the action cabinet is being asked to consider … Consequently the Cabinet Office pays particular attention to recommendations and conclusions to see that they are complete, concise, flow logically from the preceding text and are precise enough to form, if necessary, the basis for a cabinet minute.
>
> PM&C, 1994:33

The Commonwealth does not follow such procedures with cabinet minutes, though the cabinet secretariat uses colour coding within cabinet folders to distinguish cabinet committee decisions from matters requiring cabinet consideration (PM&C, 1994:43).

The record of cabinet's decisions is direct and to the point. A minute is framed in terms of submission recommendations — 'Cabinet decided to increase spending on rural drought assistance by $24 million in the coming financial year, subject to no break in current weather patterns.' It is imperative, therefore, that officers preparing submissions frame recommendations so they make sense when distributed as decisions.

As with submissions, access to cabinet decisions is also governed by security considerations. Very sensitive decisions, such as those with important defence or trade implications, may be circulated only to senior ministers, or not at all. In any case, all cabinet decisions must be secured using prescribed filing procedures. They are returned to the cabinet secretariat on a change of government, when the records of the outgoing administration are collated and locked away.

## Executive council

While cabinet is the truly powerful decision making body, Commonwealth and state constitutions vest formal authority in an executive council. It is this body that proclaims legislation, appoints people to statutory positions, changes administrative arrangements, and endorses international treaties.

The Federal Executive Council is the governor-general and the ministers. It is also known as 'the governor-general in council'. All ministers are sworn in as executive councillors, and so known by the title 'Honourable'. State executive councils are the governor and ministers, and are called 'the governor in council'. The state bodies often meet weekly, while the Federal Executive Council, chaired by the governor-general, generally meets fortnightly at Government House in Canberra. Ministers are rostered to attend. Convention dictates that at least two executive councillors are required to provide a quorum (Howard, 1996:8).

As with cabinet submissions, there is a specified format for material being presented to executive council. This is set out in a federal *Executive Council Handbook*. The governor-general may seek assurances about recommendations in an executive council minute and may decline to approve the minute until further information is provided. Such interludes are rare; executive council is essentially a constitutional formality rather than a deliberative meeting.

Protocol requires that decisions requiring the approval of the governor-general in council are not announced until it has met.

---

**Extract from the Australian Constitution**

**61.** The executive power of the Commonwealth is vested in the Queen and is exercisable by the governor-general as the Queen's representative, and extends to the execution and maintenance of this Constitution, and of the laws of the Commonwealth.

**62.** There shall be a Federal Executive Council to advise the governor-general in the government of the Commonwealth, and the members of the council shall be chosen and summoned by the governor-general and sworn as executive councillors, and shall hold office during his pleasure.

**63.** The provisions of this Constitution referring to the governor-general in council shall be construed as referring to the governor-general acting with the advice of the Federal Executive Council.

---

Although cabinet officers may take notes during discussion for the purpose of writing up minutes, they do not keep a verbatim record of discussions. Cabinet meetings are essentially without record.
PM&C, 1994:14

## Cabinet

Making cabinet decisions is a complex business. Most submissions take some weeks to work through the precabinet phase, to find a place on the agenda and then to be considered and settled. Public servants, ministers and advisers complain at times about the elaborate procedures, secrecy and ritual of cabinet deliberations. However, such routines are an important control mechanism. They introduce rigour. They spare cabinet from incomplete or inappropriate submissions. Routines ensure sufficient minimum information before a topic is discussed. They structure decision making, creating a sequence that invites analysis of proposals from a range of perspectives. Finally, cabinet rules establish clear responsibilities for implementation, making decisions the specific responsibility of particular ministers and agencies.

Through cabinet routines, governments pursue consistency. By bringing all proposals to the same meeting of ministers, and requiring information about objectives, finances, legal, regulatory, environmental, social and administrative consequences, proposals can be compared and tested. Ministers can use cabinet processes to demonstrate how a submission fits with government's overall strategy, and how its recommendations will be promoted to the community, interest groups and the media. A cabinet that works well is essential if a government is to survive politically.

## Sample cover page for a cabinet submission

This sample cover page illustrates the information required before a submission can go to cabinet. The format is drawn from the Commonwealth *Cabinet Handbook* (PM&C, 1994:70ff). Note this would be followed by the body of the submission, spelling out each of the topics covered in greater detail, and by attachments containing necessary technical and financial data.

| | |
|---|---|
| Submission Number | 300056 [ASSIGNED BY CABINET SECRETARIAT] |
| Copy Number | 1 |
| Title | REVIEW OF TERTIARY EDUCATION CHARGES |
| Minister | Senator Scott Free<br>Minister for Employment, Education, Training and Youth Affairs |
| Purpose | • To establish a review of current charges for Australian university students |

|  |  |
|---|---|
|  | • To announce no further fee increases until this review is complete |
| Program Context | • The Higher Education Contribution Scheme (HECS) is administered by the Higher Education Funding Branch of DEETYA |
|  | • This review will test the viability of sustaining current HECS charges |
| Relation to Existing Policy | • HECS was introduced with the *Higher Education Funding Act* 1988 |
|  | • HECS charges were expanded significantly in the 1995/96 budget. Overall the HECS charge represents about 23 per cent of the cost of a higher education course, although actual course costs vary between 13 per cent for medicine and 36 per cent for arts |
|  | • While current budget strategy assumes revenue from HECS, there are mounting problems with payment and evidence of disincentives to study. A review of the Scheme may improve long term viability |
| Sensitivity/Criticism | • The current operation of HECS is attracting criticism from students, parents and higher education institutions |
|  | • A freeze on further fee increases pending a review is likely to attract support from the National Union of Students (NUS) and Australian Vice-Chancellors' Committee (AVCC) |
|  | • No public consultation has occurred, pending cabinet consideration of this sensitive issue |
| Legislation Involved? | • No legislation is required at this stage. Review findings may require modification of the *Higher Education Funding Act* 1988 |
| Urgency: critical/ significant dates | • As current Year 12 students consider post-education options, the annual cycle of criticism over HECS charges has resumed |
|  | • Recent media reports have highlighted alleged inequities in the present operations of HECS |
|  | • A review must be established this month if a report is to be available for consideration in the next budget round |
| Consultation: ministers/ | • Finance |
|  | • ATSIC |
|  | • Prime Minister and Cabinet |
|  | • Australian Taxation Office |
| Is there Agreement? | • No. Finance says the matter should be considered in budget context |
|  | • Yes. ATSIC indicate concerns about current Scheme for disadvantaged students and support a review |
|  | • No. Prime Minister and Cabinet acknowledge state concerns as expressed at COAG, but do not consider the issue critical |

The Decision

|  |  |
|---|---|
|  | • Yes. Australian Tax Office acknowledges present collection difficulties and supports a review |
| Evaluation Strategy Agreed | • Yes. Though Finance does not favour a review outside the budget context, it has agreed on a methodology and appropriate measures should such a review proceed |
| Timing/handling of announcement | • No announcement is anticipated until the prime minister has approved membership of a review committee |
|  | • Once membership is settled, a review would be announced by the minister during a forthcoming national conference on higher education |
| departments consulted | • A draft media release is included at Attachment A |
| Cost:<br>• this fiscal year<br>• year 2 | • A review must be completed before Expenditure Review Committee deliberations resume in February if the findings are to be considered in the context of the next budget |
| • year 3<br>• year 4 | • Consequently, a one-off expenditure of $1.23 million is proposed, to be supplied from within the current resources of DEETYA. All money would be expended in the current financial year |

# Chapter 10

# Implementation

When cabinet has made its decision, the policy cycle moves to implementation. People are informed of the choice, policy instruments are created and put in place, staff instructed, services delivered, money spent, bills prepared for parliament. The machine of government smoothly implements cabinet's wish — in theory.

The story of implementation does not always run so well. The gap between intention and outcome may be large. Implementation failures in the pubic sector are the stuff of political debate, and quickly identified by political opponents and the media alike as examples of government incompetence.

To avoid this embarrassment, implementation issues must be considered long before a submission gets to cabinet. The rigours of the real world are the ultimate test of a policy. Poor design means a policy will fail once implemented. Consequently, a submission that has not identified the appropriate policy instruments or the necessary resources for successful implementation should not be put before cabinet. Implementation begins with policy analysis, and must carry through to recommendations for practical, achievable programs.

> **Snapshot**
> Good policies are meaningless unless implemented. Policy analysts must consider implementation needs early in the development of a proposal.
>
> This chapter explores implementation methods, and some familiar pitfalls. Advisers should develop implementation plans during policy development to enable timely implementation once cabinet approves the policy.

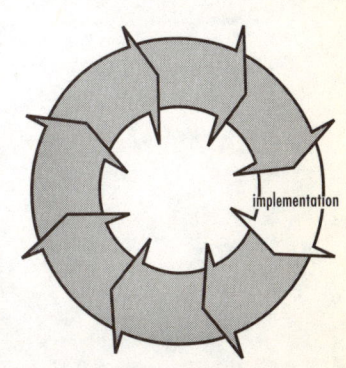

## Policy design includes implementation

Despite occasional policy failures and the practical problems of design, public policies are intended to achieve their objectives. The task of the policy adviser includes identifying implementation and design problems, and developing strategies to meet these.

The challenges are many. Of particular importance is the division of authority between multiple, sometimes competing agencies, differing objectives within government and the complexities of a federal system.

> **Ten conditions for perfect implementation —**
> 1. no crippling external constraints
> 2. adequate time and resources
> 3. a suitable combination of resources at each stage
> 4. a valid theory of cause and effect
> 5. direct links between cause and effect
> 6. a single implementation agency, or at least a dominant one
> 7. understanding and agreement on the objectives to be achieved
> 8. a detailed specification of tasks to be completed
> 9. perfect communication and coordination
> 10. perfect obedience
>
> Lewis Gunn, 1978

Noting these formidable constraints, some argue that public policies are largely doomed to fail. Academic studies have indeed found a high rate of implementation misfires, either because the policy design was fundamentally flawed, or because government agencies lacked sufficient expertise and resources. It is one thing for politicians to promise, another for government agencies to deliver.

In science no experiment is wasted — there is always something to learn. Pressman and Wildavsky's influential study *Implementation* (1973) focused on failure, but it inspired further studies and a series of important findings. Public policies will indeed fail if not designed carefully, with an eye to the many constraints on government action. Yet, through skilful analysis, evaluation and evolution, policy programs can improve over time and eventually meet their objectives. Policies are hypotheses that improve through testing and refinement.

## Conditions for successful implementation

A range of factors influence policy implementation. Along with broad contextual matters such as economic, social and political conditions, Howlett and Ramesh (1995:154–55) note that implementation is affected by —

- the nature of the problem
- the diversity of problems being tackled by government
- the size of the target group
- the extent of behavioural change required.

Those with implementation responsibility must work within cabinet objectives, available resources and competing priorities. Fortunately a vast literature suggests a few key lessons for successful implementation (Ingram, 1990:462; Davis and Weller, 1993:17) —

- all policies are built on implicit theories about the world and how it operates. If these theories are mistaken about cause and effect, the policy will fail. If, on the other hand, the model is simple, robust and tested through experience, then a policy can prevail
- policies should include as few steps as possible between formulation and implementation. The more complex the policy sequence, the more likely misunderstanding or competition will arise, with deleterious effects

- policies frequently fail if responsibility is shared among too many players. This is particularly a problem in federal systems. As more agencies become involved, the complexity of coordination overwhelms the original policy intent. A successful policy therefore will be implemented by just one or, at most, a small number of agencies

- there must be a clear chain of accountability. One person or agency must have responsibility for the success of the program, and a capacity to intervene when implementation runs into difficulties

- those who deliver a program should be involved in policy design. 'Street level bureaucrats', the people who provide the service to customers, must be informed, enthusiastic and cooperative if a program is to work

- continuous evaluation is crucial if a policy is to evolve and become more effective. As Sabatier (1988:131) notes, 'numerous studies have shown that ambitious programs which appeared after a few years to be abject failures received more favourable evaluations when seen in a longer time frame; conversely, initial successes may evaporate over time'

- policy makers should pay as much attention to implementation as to policy formulation: 'implementation cannot be divorced from policy. There is no point in having good ideas if they cannot be carried out'. (Pressman and Wildavsky, 1973:143)

## Implementation instruments

The selection of policy instruments will largely dictate the mode of implementation. Early in the policy cycle, cabinet will have considered how it wished to address a problem and therefore, by implication, the implementation instruments to be used. The cabinet submission may, for example, recommend the use of legislation or changes in government spending. Such instruments are often specifically mentioned in the cabinet minute ('cabinet decided to approve the introduction to parliament of the *Recognition of Overseas Tertiary Qualifications Bill*'). However, cabinet will rarely consider the implementation instruments in great detail, leaving discretion to individual ministers and agencies. Further, there will often be more than one implementation instrument required for successful implementation, even for relatively simple policies. If cabinet alters the original submission recommendation, or provides a lesser level of resources, an agency may need to rethink the choice of policy instruments.

There are numerous instruments open to government when planning implementation (see the useful categorisation by Anderson, 1994:214ff). Table 10.1 provides examples based on coercive and noncoercive categories of implementation instrument.

The choice of instrument is inevitably a judgement about factors such as cabinet intention, available resources, the policy target group, the risks of failure and any likely constraints on particular courses of action, such as an overall

**Table 10.1** Implementation instruments

*Noncoercive forms of action*

| | |
|---|---|
| communication | press releases, advertisements, brochures, community meetings, staff training, instruction manuals — these all communicate the policy to affected individuals and groups |
| contracts | legal agreements to regulate the private provision of government services |
| expenditures | the purchase by government of goods, services, equipment, land and other resources, and engaging staff to achieve policy objectives |
| inspection | the examination of premises, products or records to test whether these conform to officially required standards |
| loans, subsidies and benefits | making public resources available to citizens or businesses for specific purposes |
| market operations | government involvement in a market to buy, sell or provide goods |
| service delivery | provision by government of services to the public, sometimes accompanied by enforceable rights |
| taxation incentives | taxation benefits can be used as an incentive to sanction or encourage particular types of behaviour from citizens or corporations |

*Coercive forms of action*

| | |
|---|---|
| licensing | government authorisation to engage in a business or profession |
| legislation and regulation | use of laws to sanction or proscribe particular forms of behaviour. These are sometimes particular, such as licences to do certain things that are otherwise prohibited, and sometimes more general, such as the criminal law |
| administrative directions | binding directions to public servants about how they must conduct themselves, or the services they are to provide |
| reporting | mandatory requirements on corporations to report on aspects of operations and performance |
| taxation | taxation can be used to direct private activity in particular directions, and to extract returns for government from particular forms of economic activity |

government preference for markets over regulation (see Linder and Peters, 1989). Ideally cabinet will make this calculation when it accepts or modifies a policy submission. In practice, departments often find themselves drawn into the decision as they seek to turn general instructions into specific programs.

Often new policies require new organisational arrangements — either programs within a department or whole agencies. In Table 10.2 the major available program delivery choices are outlined. Each serves a specific purpose. Since the development of endless new institutions can cause coordination and accountability problems for government, it is important that policy design work only reach for such solutions when more modest avenues, such as incorporation of the new service within existing programs, are not feasible.

## Implementation traps

Just as the conditions for successful policy implementation can be identified, so there are recognised traps which can bring policies and programs to grief. Charles Lindblom (1980:65ff) identifies some of the most common. All relate to the agencies that must implement policies, and the risk that program objectives will be lost amid bureaucratic politics.

### *Incomplete specification*

Policies are rarely complete, able to cover every contingency. They must allow some discretion to those who implement and operate the program. If policy objectives are too vague, however, agencies find them difficult to implement. The result may be a policy that pursues objectives not intended by cabinet, or that wastes resources because those responsible cannot be certain what was intended.

The information required in cabinet submissions is designed to overcome incomplete specification. Nonetheless, often issues not contemplated by ministers arise during implementation, because matters of detail are rarely considered by cabinet but left to individual ministers and their departments to realise.

### *Inappropriate agency*

The selection of agency will affect the expertise available and the way a policy is delivered.

Government agencies have characteristic ways of running programs, often determined by the training and outlook of

**Table 10.2** Implementation choices — program delivery

| Delivery mechanism | Characteristics | When appropriate | Example |
|---|---|---|---|
| Departmental program | • staffed by public servants<br>• funded by consolidated revenue and/or fees<br>• located in government offices | • when the service is too complex and interrelated with other services to be specified in a commercial contract<br>• when accountability and confidentiality requirements are essential<br>• when commercial suppliers are not available<br>• when legal authority cannot be delegated | • policy advice<br>• contract monitoring of commercial suppliers<br>• child protection services<br>• administration of cash transfer programs |
| Statutory authority | • program delegated to a statutory body, often with its own legislation<br>• public sector employees<br>• funded by consolidated revenue or commercial income | • regulatory bodies, and agencies that must make judicial or quasi-judicial decisions<br>• when independence from ministerial control is required for public confidence<br>• when independent advice is required | • courts, regulatory authorities, commissions of inquiry<br>• Australian Broadcasting Corporation<br>• environmental protection agencies |
| Government owned enterprises | • commercial operations established under legislation<br>• minister remains the sole shareholder<br>• not subject to taxation but pay equivalent dividends<br>• public sector workforce<br>• commercial accounting regimes<br>• subject to public sector accountability measures and equity targets | • for business units providing services for which commercial alternatives are available<br>• for functions in transition to private ownership<br>• for testing internal provision against market costs | • agencies supplying accommodation, vehicles and cleaning for government departments<br>• large utilities<br>• organisations such as universities relying on public and private income |
| Government owned companies | • fully commercial operations in which government is a shareholder<br>• established under company law<br>• run by a board of directors<br>• private sector workforce<br>• subject to standard taxation and fiduciary arrangements | • becoming rare, but used when government has acquired an asset from private hands<br>• when privatisation is inappropriate because of natural monopoly considerations<br>• when competition is required in a market | • until recently Qantas, the Commonwealth Bank and Australian National Line were the best known national examples |
| Contracting | • government specifies product to be supplied, and awards contracts through a tender process<br>• performance monitored by public service<br>• may be one-off or a rolling contract | • when business or non-government organisations can supply goods at cheaper rates than the public sector<br>• for short-term projects<br>• when government does not wish to invest in necessary capital infrastructure<br>• when necessary skills are in short supply | • computer services for government departments<br>• case management for the unemployed<br>• major building and road construction |

the core professional workforce (Taylor, 1993). A poor choice of agency can undermine policy objectives. Education departments, for example, are set up to teach on school sites within school hours. This makes sense for many child-based activities but may be inappropriate for particular needs, such as early intervention programs for young children with intellectual disabilities. A welfare department, on the other hand, is experienced in delivering home-based services and may be better suited to the task. Cabinet decisions must be clear about who is responsible — and will be held accountable for — implementation.

## Conflicting objectives

All governments have multiple objectives, and these may be written into policy proposals. Australian Aid Abroad, for example, has humanitarian objectives, but also supports diplomatic efforts, promotes Australian technology and develops new markets. How should these be ranked and acted upon?

Usually the implementation agency must settle on operating principles. Conflicting objectives however can bring ministers and departments into dispute, as each stresses the objective they seek from the policy, potentially at the expense of overall coherence and effectiveness.

## Incentive failures

Those in agencies have some discretion about which tasks to emphasise. Without sufficient incentive to implement carefully and thoroughly, policies can fail through neglect. Implementation requires a high priority from the agency, and strategies to communicate the benefits of a new policy direction. This trap is even more common when implementation is handed over to non-government bodies, whose private or community concerns may conflict with the government's public purpose. Mandatory reporting of equal opportunity achievements is but one example of this clash.

## Conflicting directives

Those who must implement a policy are often subject to conflicting instructions. Public servants may, for example, be told to cut budgets and staff numbers by cabinet, yet to expand existing service delivery programs by clients and government. Policies are more likely to come to grief when the priorities of the agency are not clear to all involved.

---

Policies fail because —
- agencies lack the necessary expertise or commitment
- implementation mechanisms are too rigid and unwieldy
- people do not respond to the program in ways government expects
- the cost of realising the policy objective becomes too great
- the program assumes federal cooperation which does not occur
- the program assumes powers which are beyond government's control
- there are too few incentives to encourage compliance
- those implementing the program do not understand what is required.

Policies or programs fail because either the program could not be implemented as designed (program failure), or the program was run as designed but did not produce the desired result (theory failure).

Patton and Sawicki, 1993:365.

> **Studies in failure**
>
> The classic study in the field — *Implementation* by Jeffrey Pressman and Aaron Wildavsky (1973) — inclines to a pessimistic view of government capacity. *Implementation* stresses the difficulties of planning programs in the national capital for delivery in far and distant places. In this case, economic development and employment programs targeting inner-city, black residents of Oakland failed to deliver their desired outcomes. People did not get jobs. Minority businesses did not flourish. The abandoned streets of Oakland did not return to life.
>
> Pressman and Wildavsky found two principal causes for this distressing result. First, the policy was flawed. Its assumptions about how and why businesses hire turned out to be wrong. Second, the program required close cooperation between a wide array of government and private agencies. Despite good intentions, this teamwork was not achieved.
>
> Even under the best of circumstances, conclude the disappointed authors, successful implementation of public policies is 'exceedingly difficult'.
>
> Pressman and Wildavsky, 1973:xiii

### Limited competence

Many political objectives do not sit comfortably with agency capacity. An instruction to stamp out prostitution, for example, is difficult for the police to implement, even if accompanied by additional resources. Studies observe that when faced with an impossible policy objective, administrators tend to ignore official instructions and to pursue their own policy preferences.

### Inadequate administrative resources

Cabinets sometimes announce new policies without providing adequate funds. Agencies must either find the money elsewhere (and so cripple some existing program), or doom the new policy to failure through insufficient funds or expertise.

### Communication failures

Many policies rely on cooperation between government agencies and their clients. If the purpose of policy change is not explained carefully to the public sector workforce, and to those they serve, the policy is unlikely to achieve the necessary levels of commitment.

If any of these faults occurs, decision makers will not get the policy they want. Instead, agencies will be drawn into policy making, scaling down and redesigning the program. When cabinet makes symbolic gestures about a problem without providing precise instructions, a clear ranking of priorities or the right incentives and resources, it ensures implementation cannot succeed. When agencies allow too much discretion, a policy can be subverted from within, intentionally or by mistake. On the other hand, if discretion is too limited, and instructions are too rigid, policies may be implemented literally but without sensitivity to objectives or context.

## Designing an implementation strategy

Understanding why implementation succeeds or fails makes it possible to develop a strategy for implementation. While every cabinet decision is unique, there are common issues that require attention. A systematic approach to implementation improves the prospects of successful translation from cabinet minute to agency program.

A proper implementation of a complex policy will involve its own cycle, as problems are identified and analysed, options developed, consultation undertaken and decisions made.

The cycle will, for example, ensure new programs have appropriate administrative support to handle issues such as information flows, client consultation, reporting mechanisms, internal delegation appeals and approvals, and necessary publicity.

Chapter 13 offers a checklist of considerations to be kept in mind when implementing a policy decision, including the resources required for policy implementation.

Using checklists such as these provides a simple but systematic approach to implementation. Otherwise, implementation can prove the stumbling block for government. Great ideas may make hopeless programs.

The temptation for politicians is to blame program failure on the public service, but the fault more usually resides with poor policy design. Here ministers and their advisers are likely to share the fault. They can reduce the risk through a policy cycle that insists on systematic use of analysis, review and reconsideration.

Ideally, a policy will be based on a thoroughly tested model of cause and effect, with agreement about policy objectives; a central role for a single agency which is able to learn and adapt; staff commitment to the program; and regular evaluation.

Special complexity arises in a federal system. More players come into the field, each with their own reporting lines and agency objectives. The nature of policy design must change to reflect these circumstances. A bottom-up process of negotiation between interests, greater local participation, and a willingness to live with some inconsistency and overlap, may be required (Sabatier, 1986). The success of implementation rests on the skill of policy makers, and their capacity to produce viable, realistic objectives which will translate into sustainable programs.

Policies often become more effective over time because politicians, managers and agencies reflect on implementation. This is a process of 'policy learning'. It uses the lessons of implementation to reshape and refine a program (Majone and Wildavsky, 1984:170). As Lindblom (1980:65) perceptively observes, 'implementation always makes or changes policy in some degree'.

---

**Why public policies may not have their intended effect —**
- inadequate resources may be provided for implementing a policy
- policies may be administered so as to lessen their potential effect
- public problems are often caused by a multitude of factors, but policy may be directed at only one or a few of them
- people may respond or adapt to public policies in a manner that negates some of their influence
- policies may have incompatible goals that bring them into conflict with one another
- solutions for some problems may involve costs and consequences greater than people are willing to accept
- many public problems cannot be solved, at least not completely
- new problems may arise that distract attention and action from a problem
- in a federal system policies decided at one level of government may be implemented at another.

This discussion of obstacles to effective or successful policy action should not be viewed as a counsel of despair. Many public policies and programs accomplish a great deal ... If few public problems are entirely resolved by governmental actions, many are at least partly solved or ameliorated.

James Anderson, 1994:263–65.

# Chapter 11
# Evaluation

**Snapshot**

How do we know policy choices work? Is the government getting the outcomes it wanted? Do programs offer 'value for money'?

Evaluation is the point in the cycle when the utility of policy must be questioned, and a new cycle of analysis and adjustment, confirmation or abandonment begins.

The policy cycle ends — and restarts — with evaluation. An issue has been identified, worked through, addressed in a policy proposal; a decision has been made and implemented, and is now the subject of a policy program. This turn of the cycle is almost complete.

The final step, evaluation, serves three purposes —

- it asks how well a policy, once implemented, meets its objectives
- it holds officials accountable for the implementation of a policy
- it provides important clues for future policy making.

Evaluation generates data for improved policy analysis and suggestions for making the program more effective. It assists policy learning. This is the end of the cycle and also the next beginning, the starting point for a new round of identification, analysis and decisions. Evaluation criteria should be built into the original program design.

In this context, evaluation is a tool for collecting and managing information about policies and programs. The Commonwealth Department of Finance (1994:3) suggests evaluation can assist decision makers and managers to —

- assess the continued relevance and priority of program objectives in the light of current circumstances, including government policy changes
- test whether the program outcomes achieve stated objectives
- ascertain whether there are better ways of achieving these objectives
- assess the case for the establishment of new programs, or extensions to existing programs

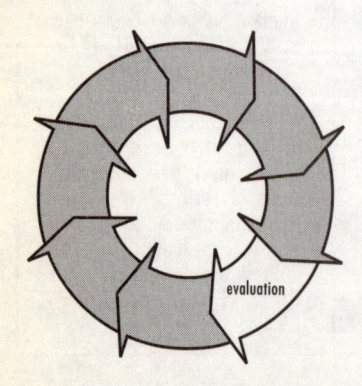

- decide whether the resources for the program should continue at current levels, be increased, reduced or discontinued.

The results should influence future policy advice and program design. A commitment to evaluation carries analytical rigour through the cycle, and emphasises that policy is iterative — an endless chain of experiments and rethinking, as policies and programs adjust to their changing circumstances.

## Evaluation and the policy cycle

Evaluation typically occurs when a policy has been implemented. The resulting program is tested for efficiency and effectiveness. Figure 11.1, developed from work by Waller (1996:11), suggests there is scope for evaluation at many points during the policy cycle.

For example, recent advice from the Commonwealth Department of Finance ('Good public policy, well delivered' is the departmental motto) stresses the importance of evaluating policy advice (see Uhr and Mackay, 1996). Policy advice is the foundation of programs; if the theory is flawed, implementation will fail. Yet interest in evaluating policy advice is surprisingly recent, and not yet systematic. A number of policy advice evaluations — known as policy performance reviews — have been able to examine inputs, process, outputs and outcomes in much the same manner as a standard program evaluation.

Agencies can also evaluate their effectiveness in briefing ministers, preparing cabinet submissions and framing recommendations. Evaluation of policy formulation and decision making assess whether ministers and managers are receiving policy advice that 'meets fully the required standards of rigour, honesty, relevance and timeliness' (Waller, 1996:9). Like all evaluations, such exercises also keep policy advisers accountable for their work.

Most evaluation work, however, focuses on the implementation stage of policy making. There is now a substantial technical literature on evaluating programs, with specialist evaluation branches in many federal and state agencies. The Commonwealth requires its programs to be evaluated every three to five years, according to a schedule set out in each department's portfolio evaluation plan. Nearly 600 evaluations have been completed under these rules, many assisted by the authoritative guide from the

> ... public policies can be evaluated at all phases of the policy-making process: in the identification and articulation of policy problems, in the formulation of alternative policy options, during the implementation of a particular policy choice, or at the termination of policy to determine its final impact. Ideally, policy evaluation provides politicians and citizens with an intelligent basis for discussing and judging conflicting ideas, proposals, and outcomes.
>
> Frank Fischer, 1995:2

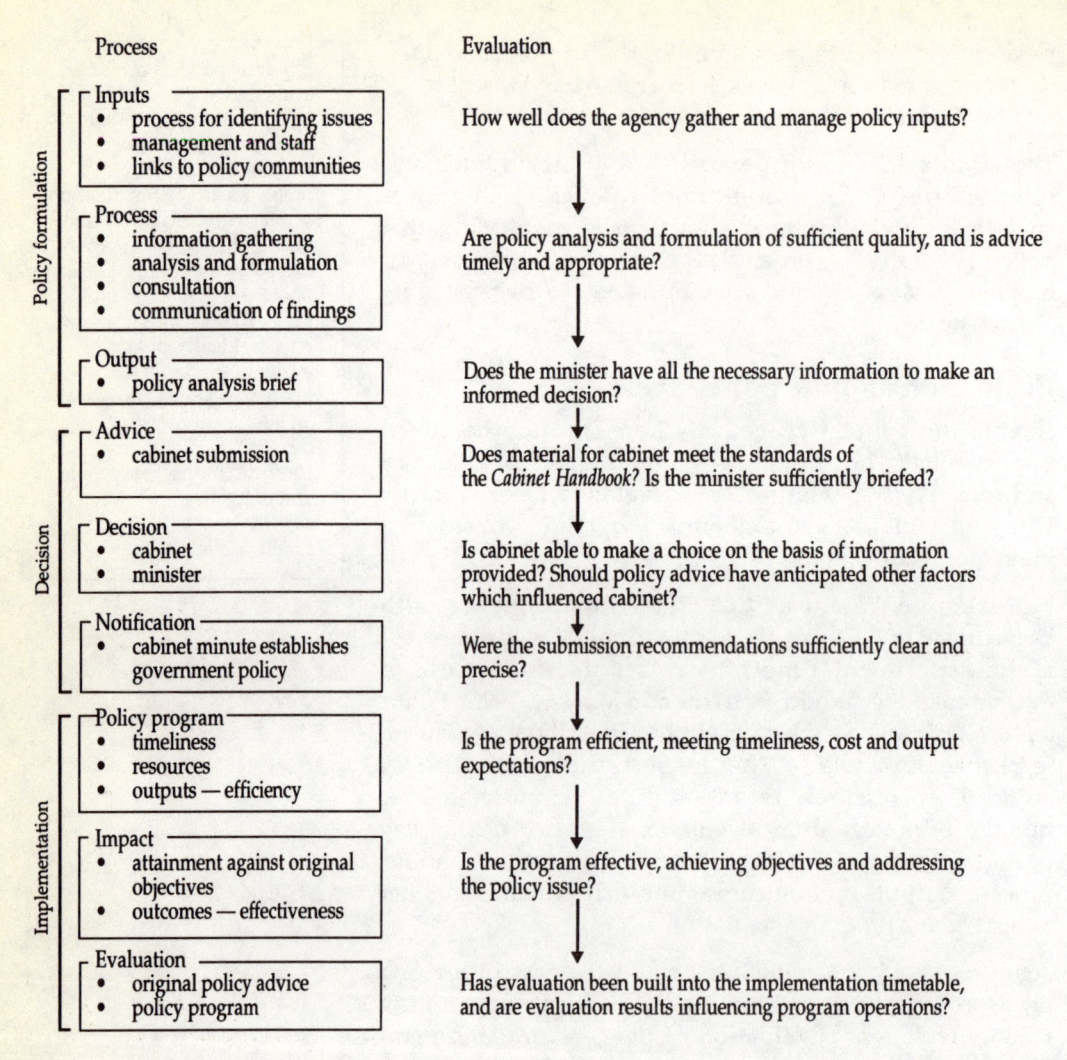

| Process | Evaluation |
|---|---|
| **Policy formulation** | |
| **Inputs**<br>• process for identifying issues<br>• management and staff<br>• links to policy communities | How well does the agency gather and manage policy inputs? |
| **Process**<br>• information gathering<br>• analysis and formulation<br>• consultation<br>• communication of findings | Are policy analysis and formulation of sufficient quality, and is advice timely and appropriate? |
| **Output**<br>• policy analysis brief | Does the minister have all the necessary information to make an informed decision? |
| **Decision** | |
| **Advice**<br>• cabinet submission | Does material for cabinet meet the standards of the *Cabinet Handbook*? Is the minister sufficiently briefed? |
| **Decision**<br>• cabinet<br>• minister | Is cabinet able to make a choice on the basis of information provided? Should policy advice have anticipated other factors which influenced cabinet? |
| **Notification**<br>• cabinet minute establishes government policy | Were the submission recommendations sufficiently clear and precise? |
| **Implementation** | |
| **Policy program**<br>• timeliness<br>• resources<br>• outputs — efficiency | Is the program efficient, meeting timeliness, cost and output expectations? |
| **Impact**<br>• attainment against original objectives<br>• outcomes — effectiveness | Is the program effective, achieving objectives and addressing the policy issue? |
| **Evaluation**<br>• original policy advice<br>• policy program | Has evaluation been built into the implementation timetable, and are evaluation results influencing program operations? |

**Figure 11.1** Opportunities for evaluation in policy formulation and implementation

Department of Finance, *Doing Evaluations: a practical guide* (1994).

## Types of evaluation

Various levels of evaluation are possible depending on the objective. Finance (1994:4) identifies four types of evaluations, each appropriate for a different step in the policy life-cycle.

*Appropriateness evaluation* helps decision makers determine whether a new program is needed, or whether an existing program should be maintained. A key question in appropriateness evaluations is the delivery mechanism — should government or the private sector deliver the service?

*Efficiency evaluation* examines how well inputs are used to obtain a given output. Is the program efficient in the way it uses public money for policy purposes?

*Effectiveness evaluation* asks whether the program is producing worthwhile results. Do the outcomes justify the expense? Is the program meeting its objectives?

Finally, *meta-evaluations* assess the evaluation process itself. Since agencies are required to evaluate programs, are their evaluation practices professional, sensitive to the social and physical environment of the program and producing reports which influence management choices?

Figure 11.2, developed by Martin and Amies (Finance, 1994:8), captures the range of evaluation types, and the information required by an evaluation team to reach a judgement.

Fischer (1995:20–21) notes that efficiency and effectiveness evaluations are more common than discussions of appropriateness, because asking about broader social

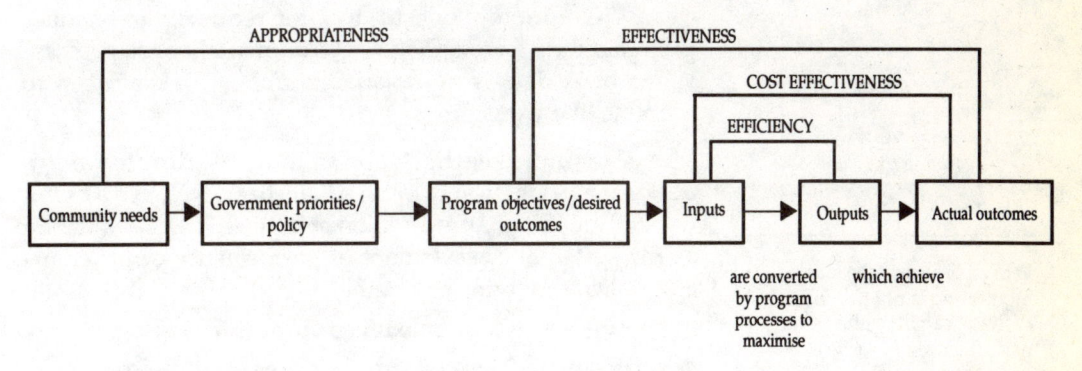

APPROPRIATENESS — The extent to which program objectives/desired outcomes align with government priorities/policy and client needs

EFFECTIVENESS — The extent to which program outcomes are achieving program objectives

COST-EFFECTIVENESS — The relationship between inputs and outcomes expressed in dollar terms

EFFICIENCY — The extent to which program inputs are minimised for a given level of program outputs, or to which outputs are maximised for a given level of inputs

**Figure 11.2** Evaluation types
(Source: Finance, 1994:8)

> **Value for money** asks 'how much input achieves how much output or what outcome?'
> - how many hip replacements were achieved within the budget?
> - how much taxpayer subsidy went to each public transport trip?
> - how many cases can be managed by a rehabilitation case worker?

interests and policy goals carries evaluation into the political realm. Even so, governments have techniques to evaluate politically sensitive policy areas, including external review committees and commissions of inquiry.

## Evaluation measures

Each type of evaluation focuses on a different measure of policy success. These are —

- *inputs* — the raw materials and resources used to deliver a policy
- *process* — the way resources are transformed into service provision
- *outputs* — the products discharged from the system
- *outcomes* — results of policy implementation for the clients and others (Kettner and Martin, 1987).

Traditional auditing counts inputs and checks compliance with process rules. Evaluation stresses outputs and outcomes: the significance of a policy lies in its impact. Only when outputs are clear can value for money questions be asked.

Outputs can often be measured, but outcomes may be elusive. It can take years for the effects of a policy to become clear. Will a more modest target for reducing greenhouse gas emissions have serious environmental consequences? When hard data is not available, policy makers need to estimate likely outcomes.

The Commonwealth Department of Employment, Education, Training and Youth Affairs has developed a useful working definition of evaluation objectives. It sees evaluation as the systematic assessment of performance of programs and policies in terms of whether —

- inputs are used to maximise outputs (*efficiency*)
- outcomes achieve stated objectives (*effectiveness*)
- objectives remain consistent with government priorities and these in turn continue to be consistent with community needs (*appropriateness*) (Crossfield and Byrne, 1994:4).

For some reviews, all three measures — efficiency, effectiveness and appropriateness — may need investigation. For other exercises with more limited objectives, a focus on efficiency and effectiveness may be more appropriate. The subject matter at hand, and the purpose of the evaluation, should define the level of analysis.

> While performance monitoring is not the only tool that can lift public sector performance, it is a very important one. We, as servants of the public, have an obligation to the community to give value for money. This goes beyond the dollars and cents of budget papers and program costings. We need to have the courage to look critically at ourselves to review how we perform and find ways to do things better.
> 
> Bill Scales, 1997:108

## Method

Evaluations tend to follow a standard format. Terms of reference are prepared for consideration by a steering committee and evaluation team. An evaluation strategy is prepared, specifying the questions to be tested and approach to be taken. Data can then be collected, and consultation undertaken with clients, stakeholders and staff. The information gathered is then analysed, leading to findings and recommendations.

In short, the evaluation process mirrors the original cycle that produced the policy; the process is iterative.

The choice of evaluation team must be consistent with the goals of the project. Many program evaluations double as an internal management review. Ideally those involved with the program are part of the evaluation, since they are in the best position to draw lessons and implement findings.

To avoid conflict of interest difficulties, agencies sometimes establish permanent evaluation branches, seconding relevant staff for a given review. When a report is likely to be contentious, agencies may even turn to external consultants. Yet the 'disadvantage of turning evaluation over to outsiders is that they lack intimate knowledge of the program, lack the experience of having seen its difficulties and savoured its successes as they were achieved' (Corbett, 1996:181).

The precise method to be followed by the evaluation team should reflect the questions to be answered. While approaches vary, and Table 11.1 is not exclusive, it is possible to link some methods with particular levels of evaluation.

**Table 11.1** Evaluation methods

| Inputs (efficiency) | Process (technical efficiency) | Outputs (effectiveness) | Outcomes (appropriateness) |
|---|---|---|---|
| • examining accounts and invoices<br>• comparing budget and actual production<br>• benchmarking with similar programs in other jurisdictions | • benchmarking to test efficiency of the production process<br>• production measures such as wastage and down time<br>• gap analysis and compliance audits | • interviews with participants and clients<br>• historical and descriptive evaluation<br>• calls for submissions from interested parties<br>• developing performance indicators | • cost-benefit analysis<br>• longitudinal research studies<br>• external policy review (such as royal commissions)<br>• long term testing against performance objectives |

> Evaluation is 'a form of practical deliberation concerned with the full range of emperical and normative issues that bear on policy judgement'.
> Frank Fischer, 1995:2

One important instrument to assist evaluation is the performance indicator. These have become an integral part of program design. Commonwealth practice requires that every new policy proposal includes a plan of action for evaluation. Performance indicators can be developed for each level of analysis, from 'the agency will deliver the program nationally within a budget of $23 million' as a general efficiency test, through to sophisticated outcome measures about, say, the expected reduction in road deaths following adoption of new safety regulations and lower speed limits.

Performance indicators allow qualified rather than absolute judgements. Few programs are unambiguous successes or failures. The typical pattern is progress toward goals, rarely complete attainment. The language of absolutes is therefore of little help. If the target for a new police initiative is 'no street crime', failure is certain. If, on the other hand, performance indicators can demonstrate a reduction in street incidents, a lower rate of reported crimes or improved public perception about safety in public places, then the same program might well be judged a success. When 'goals are stated as absolutes ... anything less than complete success tends to be construed as failure. This reading masks the real accomplishments of many public policies.' (Anderson, 1994:266)

## Findings

An evaluation must produce concise and defensible findings if it is to influence future policy design. Evaluation reports therefore resemble briefing papers offering policy analysis. They must specify the object under study, present the evidence, explore alternative explanations for the findings, and justify the particular recommendations presented.

Sometimes an evaluation process struggles to reach conclusions. Obstacles may include —
- uncertainty over policy goals
- difficulty in determining causality
- diffuse policy impacts
- difficulties in data acquisition
- resistance
- a limited time perspective (Anderson, 1994:244–50).

The fault may reside within the evaluation process, or reflect poor design in the program under scrutiny.

Recent studies of evaluation, though, argue that evaluation must live with ambiguity (Guba and Lincoln, 1989:253–56). Many social and political variables cannot be measured, yet they influence the effectiveness of government programs. Evaluation teams should see their work as collaborative exercises, a learning opportunity for all involved. The lessons generated will change the program before the evaluation is complete.

> Asked how many moves he considered before making a decision, chess master Bobby Fischer replied: 'one, the right one'.
> Tobias Jones, 1997:37

Certainly available time and methods constrain definitive judgements about much which government does; the short-term investigations of evaluation teams sit uncomfortably with the gradual accumulation of outcomes which characterises public sector activity. Still, evaluation findings remain an important moment for self-reflection, an opportunity, yet again, to begin the policy cycle.

## Evaluation

Integrating evaluation into policy design and implementation brings a certain rigour, consistent with the idea of carefully considered decisions being made by a well informed, accountable cabinet, board, executive committee or council. It means evaluation can be both the beginning, as well as the end, of the policy cycle.

Evaluation is essential if programs are to improve. Information generated through evaluation informs the next round of policy development and implementation.

Evaluation also helps keep programs adaptive and responsive. It provides a formal focus for policy learning, a way to record and share the lessons of program experience.

Persuading those offering policy advice or delivering services that evaluation is a positive can be difficult. Few people enjoy close scrutiny, or suggestions from outsiders about how to improve their performance. It takes management skill, and a professional standard of evaluation report, to maintain the commitment and enthusiasm of those subject to review.

# Chapter 12

# Managing the Policy Process

> **Snapshot**
>
> The policy process does not run itself. At each stage, ministers, their staff, policy professionals and administrators are responsible for the sequence of actions required to move policy from ideas to implementation and beyond.
>
> Those managing policy development must deal with inherent complexity, scarce resources and skills, time pressures, and conflicting roles.
>
> This chapter —
> - examines the importance of procedural integrity
> - examines ethical considerations in policy work, and
> - explores some of the management challenges in public policy and techniques available to meet them.

Public policy is the stuff of resourceful organisations: departments, statutory authorities and entire governments. It is usually multi-disciplinary, and always involves multiple players. Policy is made possible by the contribution and the interaction of those in the political, policy and administrative domains. Managing those interactions and the resources that develop, implement and evaluate policy proposals is a key challenge for ministers and for senior managers.

Policy proposals based on good quality analysis and consultation still require management. This task is necessarily divided among many officials. Policy development is not a single, continuous activity, but a set of related functions that sum to a policy cycle. At various stages, policy development may be in the hands of ministers and policy specialists (identifying a problem), line agencies (policy analysis, implementation), central agencies (coordination) or the cabinet (decision makers). Each must ensure its part of the process is done well, and flows smoothly into the next step.

Managing the public policy process is not the responsibility of one person or institution but of many. The policy cycle depends on a shared commitment to procedural integrity and professional ethics, on clear and accessible procedures, on adequate resources and appropriate structures, on delineation of roles, and on capacity to plan and complete projects.

## Procedural integrity

The substantive work of public policy — the technical and intellectual rigour that makes policy — must be complemented by a rigorous approach to procedure that ensures each domain is afforded its proper role. The policy cycle is structured by detailed procedures. Many are reflected in the Commonwealth *Cabinet Handbook* and other procedure manuals. This documentation is important, because it is often the only authoritative guide to processes which can seem otherwise disconnected and overly rule bound.

Documentation is the basis of procedural integrity — a set of rules policy players can understand and implement. In the complex world of politics, procedural integrity is a source of consistency, a way to ensure, amid political excitement, that policy development remains methodical and systematic. These documents are in fact cabinet's instructions to the players about how they must conduct themselves.

Procedural integrity means respecting policy process rules, and living within their spirit. For line departments this involves working within the framework of the *Cabinet Handbook*. It can be a long and tedious job to obtain all the data required by the cabinet submission format. But this information is all others have to evaluate a proposal or appreciate its implications. The consultation and coordination requirements are often the only way those outside government become involved, and the only way ministers can understand the views of affected individuals and groups. It is vital that these processes and records be accurate, detailed and honest.

For central agencies, procedural integrity requires consistency. The rules should be the same for all ministers and all agencies. Unless cabinet material meets the expected standard, and satisfies process rules about prior consultation, it should not go forward for consideration.

Central agencies must also document policy procedures, keep them up to date, and educate those in line departments about cabinet's requirements.

Ministers are the decision makers. For them, procedural integrity relies on 'playing by the rules' — taking policy proposals to cabinet, presenting a detailed and balanced case, and living with the decision. Ministers who leak information to the media to strengthen their hand in debate, or who insist on cabinet considering hasty and ill-prepared submissions, undermine the overall process. The breakdown of policy process rules is a reliable sign the government is divided and undisciplined.

The prime minister as chair of cabinet holds a pivotal position in the policy cycle. When prime ministers insist on procedural integrity, they signal a commitment to coherence and method in making policy choices. This comes at a cost, often offending senior ministers who expect to be excused

> Public servants need to stand up and speak out for public service. We must be more willing to extol the relative efficiency of our processes and quality of our outcomes. We should be proud that the management of our public administration is recognised internationally as progressive and innovative.
>
> Peter Shergold, 1997:124

the burdensome demands made on others. It also requires self-restraint, avoiding the temptation to dominate all choices or to resist the scrutiny imposed on the submissions of others. Prime ministers who impose strict cabinet rules risk being seen as too focused on process, too bureaucratic, and too domineering.

Yet, to be effective over the long run, government requires the consistency and coordination brought by procedural integrity to complement the technical expertise, though sometimes narrow focus, of line departments. Mike Codd (1990:10), a former Commonwealth cabinet secretary, notes the prime minister is 'guardian of the principles underlying the cabinet system'. Should cabinet processes cease to work properly, ministers become restless and the prime minister's authority is undermined.

Policy process is, of course, fallible. Clever operators get proposals into cabinet without appropriate scrutiny, citing urgency or pressing political concerns, or sometimes simply by asserting seniority. The crisis atmosphere of political life and the constant manoeuvring accentuate short-term expediency. Everyone expects, and can live with, occasional flexibility, but if the rules are broken regularly and without penalty, if routines apply to some but not others, procedural integrity is lost, and the political costs accumulate.

## Roles and ethics

The policy cycle depends on a division of labour to make sense of the complexity of government. Those involved are —

- political players — ministers and their staff, who must consider the political implications of a policy proposal
- the policy advisers — central agency officials and policy specialists within departments who provide detailed advice on submissions, coordinate government action and manage the flow of business through government
- administrators — staff in agencies who must implement and evaluate cabinet decisions, providing material for the next iteration of the policy cycle.

While good policy depends on close working relationships between these groups, the different objectives of political staff and public officials must be respected. Australia's tradition of a professional and impartial public service defines the acceptable limits of involvement by policy

> We retreat from public ethics to private ethics, as though our task were to inculcate private virtue, when in fact it is to try and institutionalise public accountability, to prepare officials for the responsible carriage of their public accountabilities, and for being assessed as a public asset.
>
> John Uhr in EARC, 1992:27

> Almost every decision taken by a public sector manager has an ethical dimension.
>
> David Corbett, 1996:218

advisers and administrators in the policy process — even if this tradition is under siege in some places.

There is an 'ethic of role' that governs behaviour in office (see EARC, 1992:21–28). Ministers and their staff subject policy advice and implementation proposals to intense political scrutiny. They ask: 'Is this proposal a sensible move for the government? What are the implications for marginal electorates? Are there more politically sensitive ways to proceed?' These are legitimate questions to ask about policy; indeed they are the political concerns ministers and their staff are employed to pursue. Policies are about political objectives.

The ethic of political office also requires restraint. Ministers may reject advice on political grounds, but cannot demand that public servants do political work, such as writing speeches for party political events, giving political advice or surveying citizens for political opinions. Nor should ministers become involved in the internal administration of an agency, particularly on matters such as staff selection. The minister's political agenda is supported by the ministerial office, not by the department.

Officials too have an ethic of role. The landmark report on the conduct of public officials by Queensland's Electoral and Administrative Review Commission (1992:16) identifies the traditional roles expected of public officials when serving governments. These are an expectation of loyal and honest service, care not to undermine public confidence in the government or its members, responsiveness and accountability, integrity, diligence, economy and efficiency.

This ethic of role imposes important obligations on policy officials. They must provide advice 'without fear or favour'. Policy advisers avoid involvement in political deliberations within government. They respect the confidentiality of cabinet deliberations, including those of previous governments. Above all, officials accept the right of elected ministers to make the final decision.

These distinct roles ensure continuity for the policy system. When ministers or governments change, public officials remain to provide advice and administrative support to the new team. A policy cycle based on recognition of different contributions can thus endure, offering each government an opportunity for discipline and coherence in decision making.

> **Frank and fearless advice**
> Ministers and chief executives need the benefit of advice offered 'without fear or favour' — advice which is tough-minded, objective and, if necessary, unpalatable.
>
> If the advice is not taken, officials should ensure the warning has been heard, then respect the right of ministers to make the final choice.
>
> As one official said of working with Commonwealth ministers, 'to object once is obligatory, twice is necessary, three times is suicidal'.
>
> quoted in Pat Weller and Michelle Grattan, 1981:83

> When a government creates a bureaucracy peopled by its own supporters, or by staff who are intimidated into providing politically palatable advice, the Government is effectively deprived of the opportunity to consider the full range of relevant factors (including but not confined to political considerations) in making decisions.
>
> Tony Fitzgerald, 1989:130

## Planning projects

Planning for public policy is partly structured by the cabinet process. The information required for a cabinet submission, along with consultation rounds, central agency negotiation, cabinet's decision and then implementation, provides a regular sequence to policy making.

Despite the rhythm of these procedural requirements, managers responsible for policy development are inevitably rushing between projects. Priorities compete for attention. Ministers need information now. 'Urgent' takes precedence over 'important'.

Managers develop routines for each step of the cycle to keep things moving. These 'routines within routines' evoke a familiar, systematic approach for every new policy problem, allowing a degree of standardisation of the unfamiliar. Managers stay in control by learning to plan projects according to a standard, proven methodology.

To take just one example of a routine for policy work, consider the actions necessary for the evaluation step of the policy cycle. The Department of Finance (1994:27) suggests a simple sequence for undertaking a policy evaluation —

*Organising the evaluation*
- organise the evaluation personnel

*Planning the evaluation*
- agree the broad terms of reference for the evaluation
- identify and consult stakeholders
- think through the program and the evaluation
- develop financial and time budgets
- prepare the evaluation strategy

*Implementing the evaluation*
- undertake the evaluation
- draft the report
- circulate the draft report before finalisation
- produce and release the report

*Controlling the evaluation*
- review the conduct of the evaluation.

A manager who followed this logical and systematic project plan should produce a thorough evaluation report. The steps take the manager through each essential task, from defining

---

**Fortune versus planning**

I am disposed to hold that fortune is the arbiter of half our actions, but that it lets us control roughly the other half.

I compare fortune to one of those dangerous rivers that, when they become enraged, flood the plains, destroy trees and buildings, move earth from one place and deposit it in another. Everyone flees before it, everyone gives way to its thrust, without being able to halt it in any way. But this does not mean that, when the river is not in flood, men are unable to take precautions, by means of dykes and dams, so that when it rises next time, it will either not overflow its banks or, if it does, its forces will not be so uncontrolled or damaging.

Niccolo Machiavelli [1513], 1988:85

the objective through organising the necessary staff, planning and executing each step of the process, producing a report, implementing its findings, and then reviewing the whole process and learning from the experience.

Similar approaches can be developed for other steps in the policy cycle. All seek to identify the task at hand, the resources and time required, and the sequence to be followed. The objective is not elaborate plans, but simple and regular processes ensuring proper consideration at each stage of the policy cycle.

A number of standard planning tools can assist managers plan policy projects. Among the most familiar is a Gantt chart, used to sequence activities, allocate resources and budget time. Key achievement points ('milestones') mark completion of significant sub-tasks, allowing a complex project to be divided into attainable portions.

| Task | Project week ||||| 
|---|---|---|---|---|---|
| | 1 | 2 | 3 | 4 | 5 |
| Task A | ▨ | ▨ | | | |
| Task B | | ▨ | ▨ | | |
| Task C | | | ▨ | ▨ | |
| Task D | ▨ | ▨ | | | |
| Task E | | ▨ | ▨ | | |
| Task F, etc. | | | ▨ | ▨ | ▨ |

**Figure 12.1** A sample Gantt chart
(Source: Department of Finance, 1994:31)

The 'critical path method' also helps budget time, but is more sophisticated. This method recognises that a complex sequence may be required, with some tasks completed simultaneously before the next can begin. Managers can estimate 'float' or flexible times. The critical path is the sequence of steps requiring most time to complete, and therefore likely to delay other sub-tasks. Figure 12.2 shows

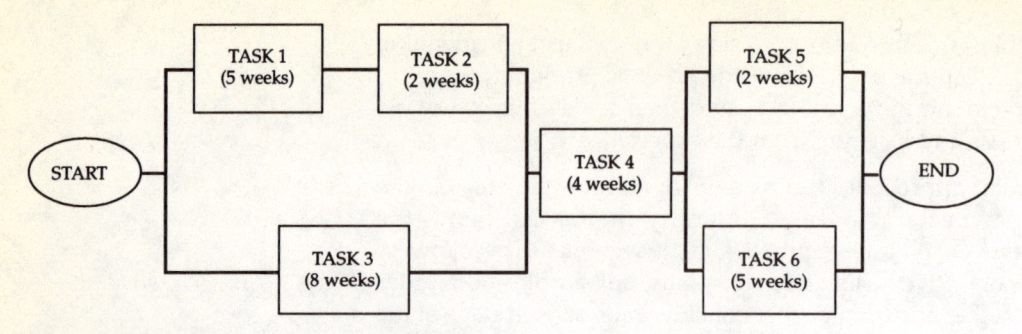

**Figure 12.2** A sample critical path chart
(Source: Department of Finance, 1994:31)

a sample critical path chart. The upper line has 'float' while the lower is the 'critical path', where tasks 3, 4 and 6 are estimated to take 17 weeks. The non-critical path (tasks 1, 2, 4 and 5) is estimated at 13 weeks.

Managers must make judgements about the required level of data, the resources to be dedicated to the task, and the available time lines for the project in order to plan properly. In general, the more urgent the policy task, the greater the resources required for a quality result. The methods described here are no substitute for professionalism and experience.

## Timing

One of the key judgements required of policy professionals is setting aside sufficient time for each step of the process. This will vary depending on the urgency of the matter, its complexity and size. The range of players interested in the decision is a major determinant of complexity. In a few urgent cases, cabinet submissions are prepared, discussed and passed in a matter of days. When problems emerge, for example following a court ruling on tax laws, new legislation can be sometimes drafted and presented to the parliament in a matter of days.

Most government activities, though, proceed at a slower pace. This is necessary if each step of the policy cycle is to receive the attention required, and to be completed to a satisfactory standard.

For a typical policy issue that becomes the subject of a cabinet submission, a timetable for each step in the policy cycle is illustrated in Table 12.1. While these time lines are illustrative only, the typical policy cycle takes from four months to nearly

**Table 12.1** Indicative timetable for a policy cycle

| Policy step | Process | Indicative times Short | Long |
|---|---|---|---|
| Identifying issues | • a briefing paper is prepared<br>• minister and agency agree a policy problem exists<br>• work is commissioned | 3 weeks | 2 months |
| Policy analysis | • data collected about the problem<br>• agency seeks information on responses in other jurisdictions<br>• a policy paper is prepared and considered by the agency and minister | 4 weeks | 4 months |
| Policy instruments | • potential policy instruments considered, compared, and a choice made<br>• if necessary, draft legislation prepared for consultation | 2 weeks | 5 months (drafting legislation can take longer) |
| Consultation | • discussion with relevant government agencies<br>• discussion with external interest groups<br>• intra- and inter-governmental negotiations | 4 weeks | 3 months |
| Coordination | • analysis by central agencies<br>• links to budget and legislative program established<br>• negotiation over cabinet submission<br>• clearance for inclusion on cabinet agenda | 2 weeks | 3 months |
| Decision | • consideration by cabinet<br>• decision issued as a cabinet minute | 2 weeks | 1 month |
| Implementation | • agency secures resources to act<br>• necessary legislation passed by parliament and given assent (parliamentary times depend on available sittings and are not included)<br>• subordinate legislation developed and promulgated<br>• program established and operational | 5 weeks | 6 months |
| Evaluation | • program review, report and modifications | 1 year | 1 year |
| Timing range | Time (assumes legislation takes no longer than six months to prepare, and excludes parliamentary stages) | 1 year, 22 weeks | 3 years |

two years between recognition of a problem and program implementation. Long-standing policies may go through the cycle many times, being reviewed and modified while assumptions remain unchanged.

## Management and the policy process

From the perspective of a policy manager in a line department, many people have a stake in the policy cycle —

- ministers and their political advisers
- the agency's chief executive
- the heads of the policy unit and relevant division
- the staff working on the policy issue
- the agency's cabinet liaison staff.

All expect to be consulted during the course of policy deliberations. The policy officer is likely to receive calls from —

- central agencies, particularly the PM&C and treasury
- other line agencies interested in the policy area
- groups likely to be affected by any policy change
- external groups which contribute to policy change, such as lobbyists, consultants and think tanks.

Managing the policy process requires significant judgement and people skills. John Wanna and his colleagues (1994:1.2.4) suggest policy managers must learn to manage up, across, down and out.

When *managing up*, the policy officer recognises the needs of the minister and chief executive. These people are unlikely to become involved in the detailed drafting of policy, but their views must be taken into consideration. Ultimately it is the minister who owns, and must argue for, a cabinet submission. The skill of 'managing up' is to recognise how the world looks from various standpoints. Public servants properly put great stress on operational questions, but a minister and chief executive must deal with a bigger picture — not just whether a policy can be implemented, but how it fits into the wider mosaic of government priorities. Understanding the particular concerns of those in command is important; as the saying goes, 'where you stand depends on where you sit'.

In *managing across*, policy officers deal with their peers in their own and other line agencies, and with similarly placed officers in the central agencies. Managing across is part of

> Policy is the means by which the lives of individuals, families and communities are shaped. It is the means by which we shape the character and future of the nation.
> It is the purpose of political life, the only worthwhile measure of political success, and by far the most significant measure of the worth of politicians and political parties.
>
> Paul Keating, 20 October 1995

coordination in government, the endless task of letting others know what is proposed and giving them an opportunity to comment. It means circulating drafts of policy documents and organising meetings to discuss proposals. Equally, managing across requires policy officers to respond to the requests of others for comment and ideas. In a world of networks, managing across is assuming increasing importance. Even if only connected to a 'virtual' community of peers through electronic mail and fax machines, policy managers should give time to, as well as impose on, others.

Policy managers often supervise staff. *Managing down* is not just commanding, but empathy, encouragement and appreciation of the others' contributions. General Patton was fond of saying: 'Never tell people how to do things. Tell them what you want to achieve, and they will surprise you with their ingenuity.' (Gore, 1993:12) Policy development typically requires team work. A skilful manager builds team morale and competence, delegates, and sets goals and time lines for the work team.

Finally, in a policy context, *managing out* means dealing with clients likely to be affected by policy change — community members and groups and those within the public sector responsible for delivering the program. Their cooperation may be essential to the policy achieving its objectives. Managing out often involves informing and advising about policy choices; sometimes it means organising formal consultation sessions and ensuring feedback influences policy design.

Balancing all of these tasks is a formidable task. The key skills required are shown in Table 12.2.

**Table 12.2** Management skills for policy officers

| Task | Skills |
|---|---|
| Managing up | • recognise expectations of ministers and senior officers |
|  | • anticipate requirements of ministers and senior officers |
| Managing across | • recognise extent of interest in, and impact of, issues across agencies |
|  | • encourage and be receptive to coordination |
| Managing down | • implement programs |
|  | • support and maintain personnel |
| Managing out | • respond sensitively to client needs |

(Source: Wanna et al., 1994:1.2.4)

> Any government must first learn how to govern its own organisational world before it can attempt to govern society.
> Hugh Emy, 1976:vii

## Organising for public policy

Effective public policy requires resources and organisational commitment to outcomes. Many public sector agencies have policy divisions dedicated to developing and coordinating policy proposals through the policy cycle. Other agencies, especially smaller service delivery bodies, cannot fund dedicated staff but identify officers who have the necessary skills and assign policy duties to them on a project basis. Others may have a small number of dedicated policy staff in service delivery divisions. Sometimes policy analysis is contracted out to consultants.

The need to understand the substantive area may dictate the qualifications of policy staff. But policy is multi-disciplinary, and 'professional agendas' must be managed. Qualifications in the substantive field do not necessarily make one a good policy officer; sometimes the opposite is true. Apart from experts in the substantive field, it is common for economists and lawyers to provide policy advice. Economic and legal methods still dominate policy analysis. A profession of public policy has been slow to emerge, though tertiary education institutions now include policy studies in their curricula and the Institute of Public Administration Australia has promoted more training in policy skills.

Whatever the background of policy professionals, however, it is imperative the systems established do not depend on an individual. Preparing standard operating procedures, writing procedure manuals and developing other forms of corporate memory are essential if the policy cycle is to endure. Otherwise a change in leadership or government may herald, not a smooth transition to a new set of policies, but the collapse of the routines and the personnel central to good public policy.

Sustainable systems use learning organisation principles. Information is recorded and shared; skills transferred to others; excellence nurtured and rewarded; change greeted as a challenge; assumptions tested honestly; performance measured.

Recruiting skilled staff, providing them with the right tools for their work and finding time to document and educate is costly, and often difficult in the public sector, where the traditional measures of success are more hierarchical than outcome driven.

## Professionals

Many agencies have a strong professional work force — engineers, scientists, nurses, school teachers, social workers — with skills essential for program delivery. Harnessing their expertise in policy development is a management challenge because of the potential for conflict between governmental and professional agendas. Will professionals be on tap, or on top?

Good policy process avoids this difficulty by insisting on coordination. When proposals are developed against 'whole of government' objectives, and tested with sceptical central agencies, the possibility of professional bias is reduced. The 1987 amalgamation of Commonwealth agencies into 'mega-departments' was designed in part to ensure policy proposals were considered from a range of perspectives. Combining foreign affairs and trade, for example, provides a dialogue between foreign policy and Australia's trade interests.

> There is always a risk that a consensus among professionals will crowd out other, non-professional, views. As Frank Fischer (1995:12) notes, the 'rational person' seems the one 'who agrees to submit to the properly derived technical and administrative knowledge of the scientific expert. The authority of the expert, from this perspective, ultimately takes precedence over the democratic exchange of opinions.'

Properly managed, the policy cycle brings together political, policy and administrative players in government. Professionals are an important part of the equation. Their role — like that of other advisers — is to be part of a wider process, and to accept that policy balances professional rationality with political need and administrative practicality.

## Managing the policy process

The policy cycle is a form of coordination, a way to sequence the various tasks and skills necessary for making, delivering and evaluating public policy.

To work effectively, this cycle requires procedural integrity, acceptance of differing roles, careful planning and policy officers able to manage complexity and ambiguity, so keeping the process focused.

These skills must be widely shared across government, and procedures documented. The policy cycle is not a smooth loop of assigned tasks, but a quite disjointed process with each step belonging to different players. Continuity is provided by the routines of decision making, especially those embodied in the cabinet system.

> Policy making is a daunting task — Godlike even — for in attempting to change a society we are, for better or worse, helping to create new kinds of human beings with new values.
>
> David Donnison, 1994:29

# Chapter 13
# Checklists for Policy Development

**Snapshot**
This chapter provides a summary of the policy cycle, and systematic checklists of actions required to make public policy choices.

This policy handbook is based on a policy cycle, and is designed to encourage a systematic approach to decision making. Good process cannot guarantee good policy, but it does encourage rigour and prevent elementary mistakes.

Policy making is political and hence unpredictable. Few decisions are afforded sufficient time or resources for every step in the policy cycle; most are rushed, and the pressure for ad hoc work remains great. Reality tempers the ideal of systematic policy development.

Over time, policy cycle routines and role prescriptions foster policy skills. Policy makers learn to recognise the interplay of politics, policy and administration. They become proficient at designing and testing policy options. They become sensitive to the responses of others. Preparing concise, informative briefing notes and cabinet submissions becomes a familiar activity, as do consultation and evaluation. Ministers and their advisers become familiar with the rhythms of cabinet process, the format of key documents, and the data needed for informed decisions.

Such policy skills, widely dispersed, are essential for good government. They assist a professional approach to decision making. Policy participants who value thoughtful, well argued and properly evaluated policy proposals reduce the risk of foolish choices, and of bringing government into disrepute.

Policy making is a cooperative venture between political operatives and public servants. Each domain plays to its strengths, yet they maintain separate roles. It does not help the policy process if public servants become politicised. Equally, ministers are not well served if their advisers become bureaucrats, more concerned about the technical detail than the government's political objectives.

Policy making must meld different perspectives into viable cabinet submissions and programs. These balance politics with policy, and good ideas with sound administration. Issues move back and forward across the players on their long journey from ideas to implementation.

The routines of cabinet provide some structure for the policy process, but significant discretion remains for departments to establish their own procedures. Thus, within government, each agency develops unique characteristic ways of making policy. Some stress documentation of each step. Others are more informal, relying on the skills and experience of policy officers to carry policy development through the cycle.

These differences in operating procedure do not matter if policy outputs are of high and consistent quality, and policy outcomes achieve the changes required. They may even add diversity, and with it the potential for creativity within the strictures of process.

We offer the following summary and policy checklists, knowing that even experienced policy specialists need occasionally to refresh their skills and knowledge.

Table 13.1 provides a summary of the policy process, which is then expanded in a series of checklists for developing policy objectives, offering policy advice and managing the policy cycle.

Finally, Table 13.2 provides a guide to implementing new policies. The focus here is on translating policy decisions into viable government actions. This interplay of good ideas and well designed actions, of plausible theories and thoughtful programs, is the core of good public policy.

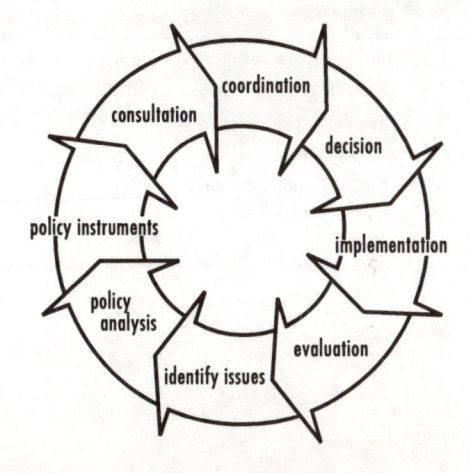

The Australian policy cycle

**Table 13.1** Summary of the policy process

| Policy cycle step | Political domain | Policy domain | Administrative domain |
|---|---|---|---|
| **Identify issues** | • search for ideas<br>• regular discussion with sources of policy advice<br>• sensitivity to emerging policy concerns | • regular advice to government about current and emerging issues | • data capture and flow |
| **Policy analysis** | • specification of policy issues and the range of choices government might consider | • briefs on policy issues and their consequences<br>• technical analysis | • data and technical support |
| **Policy instruments** | • indication of ministerial preference | • policy instrument options<br>• advice on legal issues | • data and technical support |
| **Consultation** | • stakeholder identification<br>• political level consultation | • agency stakeholder identification<br>• policy community consultation | • process support |
| **Coordination** | • ministerial office negotiations<br>• clearance of cabinet submission | • preparation of policy submission<br>• negotiations with central agencies<br>• document quality control | • financial, administrative and personnel data for the cabinet submission |
| **Decision** | • determination by cabinet | • preparation of cabinet minutes and further briefs | • action planning on basis of cabinet minute |
| **Implementation** | • minister kept informed on progress | • resource identification<br>• legal document preparation | • resource allocation and utilisation |
| **Evaluation** | • request for information<br>• political analysis of results<br>• decision about continuation | • monitoring performance<br>• analysis of data from evaluation<br>• identification of issues for next turn of the cycle | • regular evaluation, reporting of results, adjustments to program |

# Checklists

## Policy objectives

does a policy statement express a considered response to an issue? ❑

is the policy consistent with, and expressive of, government philosophy? ❑

is the policy a clear and authoritative statement of intent? ❑

does the policy provide sufficient detail to allow implementation? ❑
- implementation responsibility assigned ❑
- resources identified ❑
- implementation plan prepared ❑
- implementation project team identified and available ❑
- drafting instructions for legislative changes ❑

are the goals sufficiently precise and detailed to allow later evaluation? ❑
- costs and benefits articulated ❑
- benchmarks identified ❑
- performance criteria stated and agreed ❑

are resources available to implement the policy? ❑
- operating costs ❑
- capital costs and set up costs ❑
- is someone else required to contribute financially or in kind ❑
- staff ❑
- staff training program ❑
- office space in appropriate centres ❑
- office equipment and requisites ❑
- plant and equipment ❑
- contractors ❑
- support services ❑
- communication plan ❑

is the policy enforceable? ❏
- legally sustainable ❏
- enforcement resources identified and available ❏
- enforcement procedures identified ❏
- timely enforcement practical and achievable ❏
- sanctions and rewards relate to desired behaviour change ❏

## Policy advice objectives

will the decision maker hear about relevant issues in a timely manner? ❏

is the decision maker informed about contending opinion on the matter? ❏

are clear, different options available and presented honestly to the decision maker? ❏

does the decision maker have sufficient information to make a decision? ❏
- budget information ❏
- staff and other resource requirements ❏
- legal implications ❏
- social, environmental and other impacts ❏
- technical data ❏
- consultation and its results ❏

can the decision be tested by evaluating program performance? ❏
- performance criteria developed ❏
- benchmarks established ❏
- measurement instruments ❏
- reporting requirements established ❏

## Managing the policy cycle

are there procedure manuals to guide the policy process? ❏

are staff allocated responsibility for coordinating policy responses within the agency? ❏

are adequate skills available for well rounded analysis? ❏

is there appropriate project planning? ❑

is the need for procedural integrity, and the separation of political and policy roles, understood and built into the policy development process? ❑

is the project timetable realistic? ❑

does the project manager understand the need to manage up, across and down? ❑

have the perspectives of professionals been included in policy advice? ❑

## Policy cycle objectives

### *Issue identification*

- is there agreement on the nature of the problem? ❑
- are there feasible solutions to the problem? ❑
- is this an appropriate issue for government? ❑
- for whom in government is this a problem? ❑

### *Policy analysis*

- has the issue been accurately formulated? ❑
- are objectives and goals explicit and clear? ❑
- has the search for alternatives been thorough? ❑
- have the appropriate analytical tools been used for the issue? ❑
- have resource constraints, legal requirements and external accountability been taken into account in any policy advice? ❑
- is there a superior alternative? ❑
- has implementation been considered in policy design? ❑

### *Policy instruments*

- is advocacy, money, direct government action or law the best approach to this problem? ❑
- is this a reasonable way of proceeding in this policy area? ❑
- will the preferred instrument be cost-effective? ❑

- can this instrument get the job done? ❏
- is the instrument simple and robust, and can it be implemented? ❏

*Consultation*

- are the objectives of the consultation process clear? ❏
- has an appropriate information, consultation, partnership, delegation or control strategy been developed? ❏
- does the timetable allow sufficient scope for meaningful input and consideration? ❏
- are the resources to be committed commensurate with the importance of the problem? ❏
- have all relevant stakeholders been identified and included? ❏
- is there information available, and appropriate access to the consultation process? ❏
- have contributions been acknowledged? ❏
- has feedback from consultation been incorporated into policy advice? ❏

*Coordination*

- are proposals logical, well considered and consistent with other government initiatives? ❏
- is the required money properly targeted and fully budgeted? ❏
- have the employment, industrial, equity and fairness consequences of a proposal been worked through? ❏
- have other factors which might influence attainment of policy objectives been identified? ❏

*Decision*

- should this matter go to cabinet? ❏
- is the submission in the appropriate format? ❏
- do the recommendations provide an adequate basis for a cabinet minute? ❏
- has an implementation timetable been indicated in the submission? ❏

- have the minister and ministerial office been briefed on likely objections? ❏
- does cabinet have sufficient information to understand the consequences of its choice? ❏

*Implementation*
- is the objective clear and the underlying causal model reliable and tested? ❏
- is a top-down or bottom-up approach most appropriate to the issue? ❏
- is the assigned agency the most appropriate to implement the policy? ❏
- can implementation steps and players be kept to a minimum? ❏
- is there an agreed project leader and a clear chain of accountability? ❏
- have 'street level bureaucrats' been involved in implementation design? ❏
- has an evaluation strategy been included in the implementation plan? ❏
- is legislation necessary, and used only as a 'last resort'? ❏
- how will the policy's effect be communicated to staff and clients? ❏
- is the policy enforceable? (see Policy Objectives Checklist) ❏

*Evaluation*
- is the appropriate measurement of policy success evaluation of inputs, process, outputs or outcomes? ❏
- given the nature of the policy problem, has an appropriate level and type of evaluation been identified? ❏
- can performance indicators be developed for the program? ❏
- have evaluation findings informed the next cycle of policy advice? ❏
- should the program be continued, modified or terminated? ❏

**Table 13.2** Designing a new program

| Issue | Action |
|---|---|
| Clarify objective | • listed in cabinet submission<br>• conflicting criteria must be recognised and ranked<br>• specification of the objective is crucial, since it will form the basis of later evaluation |
| Agree on an appropriate process | • implementation can proceed through top-down or bottom-up approaches. The process should be guided by the objectives and the nature of the policy issue<br>• use a project planning methodology to map out time frames, resource requirements, milestones and reporting dates |
| Identify an implementation team leader | • cabinet minutes assign implementation responsibility to a minister and agency<br>• within the agency those managers with implementation responsibility are identified and assigned tasks<br>• to ensure accountability, implementation requires a team leader with appropriate authority to ensure follow-through |
| Create a reporting mechanism | • to monitor implementation, a sequence of regular reports is important<br>• reports should indicate progress against timetable and budget, feedback from those involved, and assessment of pending problems or opportunities |
| Identify policy instruments | • the cabinet submission will indicate the preferred policy instruments, but re-evaluation is often necessary, especially if cabinet alters the proposed recommendation<br>• the implementation team must reflect on the proposed course of action, and confirm or modify the choice of instruments |
| Identify required resources | • the original cabinet submission should include costings for the policy and identification of available resources<br>• resources should be matched with milestones, so that cash flow requirements (or other inputs) can be calculated and planned |
| Agree on a timetable and milestones | • cabinet may provide a timetable for implementation, but this is often left to the discretion of the agency<br>• time lines are crucial for project planning<br>• once an end date for implementation is settled, project planning should include 'milestones' — points along the way when specific actions must be completed<br>• reporting dates should be agreed in advance with the minister and department |
| Information systems | • identify the information necessary for this program to run, and the information technology equipment required<br>• plan information system installation to match implementation timetable |

| Issue | Action |
|---|---|
| Plant and equipment | • if delivered within government, a program will need appropriate accommodation, equipment and consumables<br>• internal responsibility for procuring and maintaining these assets must be established, with appropriate reporting and monitoring systems |
| Delegations | • if run in-house, the program will need staff and resource delegations, preferably devolved to the lowest available unit<br>• delegations and approval systems should be supported by procedure manuals and appropriate accountability documentation |
| Prepare communication plan | • implementation relies on understanding by staff and clients<br>• a new policy will therefore need a communication plan, which explains the rationale and the process for implementation<br>• this may include meetings with staff and customers, printed material, even advertising<br>• consider any special communication needs for remote areas or widely distributed staff, and for staff or clients with special communication needs (e.g. languages other than English) |
| Consultation | • the communications plan should include opportunities for feedback so that the implementation team can gauge reaction to the policy, and identify possible problem areas |
| Mark the completion of implementation | • to communicate that implementation has been completed, to acknowledge the work of the team, and to build commitment to the new program, it is often useful to mark the completion of implementation |
| Evaluation | • the implementation timetable should include an evaluation phase<br>• evaluation should be conducted by people outside the implementation team, and should test the program against the original policy objectives and budget |

# Appendix — Internet Resources for Public Policy

The Internet has enormous potential for public policy makers. At present it is used mainly for communication with other policy professionals and research of policy issues. Yet policy development, data capture, consultation and policy implementation can all find a place on the 'net'. With benefits, of course, come challenges. Amid the excitement, the net also presents a major technological development beyond the conception of many policies and laws.

This Appendix outlines basic principles of the Internet, with pointers about using its potential. The Internet is not only large but dynamic to the point of volatility: the resources included here may well be out of date before these pages are printed.

This appendix is a resource. We do not necessarily endorse the material contained on these sites. It is important to remember the net is an open exchange medium, in which the useful and the trivial, the accurate and the wildly improbable mix continually. Readers should not assume that information obtained from Internet sources is accurate or up to date, and be mindful that most Internet communication is public.

## What is the Internet?

The Internet is a collection of many computers, communicating on a global scale, defying notions of place and jurisdiction. The boundaries of Australian states, of Australia itself, are meaningless when data can flow across oceans in seconds, to be examined in homes or business or government offices by all comers.

The language of the Internet is confusing for novices, especially those from non-technical backgrounds. The acronym rules. Some of the more important acronyms are explained in Table 14.1. Sites with more explanation of the Internet, its history and operation include —

- *Glossary of Internet Terms*
  http://www.matisse.net/files/glossary.html

- *NetGlos — The Multilingual Glossary of Internet Terminology*
  http://wwli.com/translation/netglos/netglos.html

- *Feminism and the Net*
  http://www.eskimo.com/~feminist/nownetin.html

**Table 14.1** Internet Acronyms

| | |
|---|---|
| BBS | Bulletin board software |
| FAQ | frequently asked questions |
| ftp | file transfer protocol |
| html | hyper text markup language, the computer program language used to create WWW pages |
| http | hyper text transfer protocol, the protocol used for WWW pages |
| IRC | Internet relay chat |
| ISP | Internet service provider |
| NNTP | network news transfer protocol |
| POP | point of presence |
| PPP | point-to-point protocol, used for electronic mail |
| TCP/IP | transmissions control protocol/Internet protocol, the basic communication protocol of the Internet |
| SLIP | serial line Internet protocol |
| SMTP | simple mail transfer protocol |
| WWW/3W | World Wide Web, one of the major Internet 'spaces' |
| URL | uniform resource location, the 'address' of WWW pages |

## Internet components

The major components of the Internet are described briefly below. More detailed information is available from the Electronic Frontier Foundation (*http://www.eff.org/papers/eegtti/eegttitop.html*) or from InterLinks at Nova Southeastern University (*http://www.nova.edu/Inter-Links/resources.html*). Using the Internet requires a computer with modem or network linkage to an Internet server and special software.

> The worldwide Net is actually a complex web of smaller regional networks. To understand it, picture a modern road network of transcontinental superhighways connecting large cities. From these large cities come smaller freeways and parkways to link together small towns, whose residents travel on slower, narrow residential ways. The Net superhighway is the high-speed Internet. Connected to this are computers that use a particular system of transferring data at high speeds.
>
> EFF's Guide to the Internet:
> http://www.eff.org/pub/Net_info/EFF_Net_Guide/netguide.eff

**World Wide Web** (WWW), the fastest growing information and communication resource on the planet. This has space for home pages, and is increasingly where policy and legal information are accessible. WWW addresses have the format *http://domain/resource*. For example, the National Library of Australia's domain name is 'www.nla.gov.au'. Each part, separated by a dot, has a meaning: 'www' means World Wide Web, 'nla' is the National Library of Australia, 'gov' refers to the fact this is a government organisation, and 'au' is the two letter country code for Australia. The Sydney Olympic Organising Committee domain is *www.sydney.olympic.org*. (Not all Australian sites use the country code 'au'.) Resource names are usually computer files stored on the remote computer network, many in the http language, but often in other formats.

Many governments now have WWW sites. Indeed, Australian governments are among the best at providing information through the WWW, though sites tend to be static information providers rather than dynamic information exchange platforms. Political parties too maintain WWW sites, and much policy platform information is accessible from these.

WWW sites are accessed with a 'browser'—computer software that makes special use of the http language. The most widely used are Netscape Navigator and Microsoft Internet Explorer; both enable users to 'bookmark' favourite sites.

**Electronic mail** (e-mail): the means by which messages are sent through the Internet to a particular address, in the form *person@domain*. The official e-mail address for the President of the United States, Mr Bill Clinton, is *president@whitehouse.gov*. Allen & Unwin, the publishers of this book, are at *frontdesk@allen-unwin.com.au*. Using e-mail requires access to SMTP and POP servers as well as the software.

**Electronic mailing lists**: automated discussion groups that use e-mail for communicating with subscribers. A list server is software that receives and forwards on a message intended for broadcast to subscribers. Groups are either moderated (the list 'owner' vets each possible mailout) or unmoderated (all messages are sent out). Lists are an excellent way of exchanging relatively small items of information. For example, the Commonwealth Department of Administrative Services maintains a list about public sector management (pubsec@das.gov.au).

**Usenet newsgroups**: Imagine a conversation carried out over a period of hours and days, as if people were leaving messages and responses on a bulletin board. Or imagine the electronic equivalent of a radio talk show where everybody can put their two cents worth in and no one is ever on hold. Unlike e-mail, which is usually 'one-to-one', Usenet is 'many-to-many'. Usenet is the international meeting place, where people gather to meet their friends, discuss the day's events, keep up with computer trends or talk about whatever's on their mind. Jumping into a Usenet discussion can be a liberating experience. Nobody knows what you look or sound like, how old you are, what your background is. You're judged solely on your words, your ability to make a point' (Electronic Frontier Foundation, *EFF's Guide to the Internet, v. 3.20,* *http://www.eff.org/pub/Net_info/EFF_Net_Guide/netguide.eff*).

**Telnet and ftp sites** allow users to access files from a directory structure on a remote host. Telnet users actually 'log on' to the remote computer. With ftp, files are transferred using special software.

**Gopher**: software for tunnelling through the Internet, named after a North American animal with a tunnelling habit. It is a search tool, particularly useful for telnet and ftp sites. Many ftp and gopher sites are accessible through WWW browsers.

## Searching the Internet

There is a vast array of information on the internet, much of it not catalogued in any particular way, sometimes reflecting the idiosyncrasies of a site's creator. The resources listed here are mostly WWW sites, and all are free to access.

## Australian public policy resources on the Internet

### Australian governments

Australian Government Directory
http://www.agd.com.au/agdgovernment.html

Australian Government Home Page
http://gov.info.au/

The National Library of Australia
http://www.nla.gov.au/oz/gov/

Ipswich Global Information Service
http://infoservice.gil.com.au/resource/gov/

### State and territory governments

ACT
http://www.act.gov.au/

New South Wales
http://www.nsw.gov.au

Northern Territory
http://www.nt.gov.au/

Queensland
http://www.qld.gov.au/

South Australia
http://www.sacentral.sa.gov.au/government/govern.html

Tasmania
http://www.tas.gov.au/government/

Victoria
http://www.vic.gov.au/

Western Australia
http://www.wa.gov.au/government.html

### Australian parliaments

ACT
http://www.dpa.act.gov.au/ppc/SENOff1/PROGS/assemb.html

Commonwealth
http://www.aph.gov.au/house/ (House of Representatives)
http://senate.aph.gov.au/ (Senate)
http://hansard.aph.gov.au/ (Hansard)
http://library.aph.gov.au/library/ (Parliamentary Library)

New South Wales
http://www.parliament.nsw.gov.au/
http://www.parliament.nsw.gov.au/gi/hansard.html (Hansard)

Northern Territory
http://www.nt.gov.au/lant/

Queensland
http://www.parliament.qld.gov.au
http://www.parliament.qld.gov.au:81 (Hansard)

South Australia
http://www.sa.gov.au/government/sagov.htm

Tasmania
http://www.parliament.tas.gov.au/
http://www.parliament.tas.gov.au:8000/index.htm (Hansard)

Victoria
http://www.vicnet.net.au/vicnet/vicgov/parl/parlia.html
http://www.dms.dpc.vic.gov.au/pdocs/ (Parliamentary documents)

Western Australia
http://www.wa.gov.au/parl/index.html

## Australian legislation and legal resources

Australia arguably leads the world in providing its laws free of charge to citizens, businesses and visitors, using the WWW as the main vehicle. At the time of writing, Queensland and Tasmania were the only jurisdictions not to do so. The Tasmanian government has expressed an intention to make its consolidated legislation available through the Department of Premier and Cabinet at *http://info.dpac.tas.gov.au/*.

## Australian legal sites

The Australian Legal Information Institute (AustLII)
http://www.austlii.edu.au/

Foundation Law
http://www.fl.asn.au/menu.html

High Court
http://www.hcourt.gov.au/

Lawnet
http://www.lawnet.com.au/

## Australian policy and political players

### Significant political parties

Australian Democrats
http://www.democrats.org.au/

Australian Greens
http://www.peg.apc.org/~ausgreen/

Australian Labor Party
http://www.alp.org.au/

Liberal Party of Australia
http://www.liberal.org.au/

National Party of Australia
http://www.npa.org.au/

### Interest groups, peak bodies and think tanks

Aboriginal and Torres Strait Islander Commission
http://www.atsic.gov.au/

Australia Institute
http://www.ozemail.com.au/~austinst/austinst.html

Australian Conservation Foundation
http://www.peg.apc.org/~acfenv

Australians for Constitutional Monarchy
http://www.mq.edu.au/hpp/politics/acm.html

Australian Council of Social Service
http://www.acoss.org.au/

Australian Council of Trade Unions
http://www.actu.asn.au/

Australian Republican Movement
http://www.republic.org.au/

Centre for Australian Public Sector Management, Griffith University
http://www.cad.gu.edu.au/capsm/capsm.htm

Community and Public Sector Union
http://www.cpsu.org/

Council for Aboriginal Reconciliation Secretariat
http://www.austlii.edu.au/car/

Centre for Independent Studies
http://www.cis.org.au

Evatt Foundation
http://www.peg.apc.org/~evatt/welcome.html

H.R. Nichols Society
http://venue.exhibit.com.au/~nicholls/

National Farmers' Federation
http://coombs.anu.edu.au/SpecialProj/NFF/NFFHomePage.html

LeftLink (Victoria)
http://www.alexia.net.au/~www/mhutton/index.html

National Women's Justice Coalition
http://www.ozemail.com.au/~nwjc/

Samuel Griffiths Society
http://www.exhibit.com.au/~griffith

Sydney Institute
http://www.nim.com.au/sydney/

Women's Electoral Lobby
http://www.pcug.org.au/other/wel/

### Australian political resource pages

Armidale Politics Page
http://www.une.edu.au/~arts/Politics/armpol.htm

Australians Abroad politics page
http://www.coolabah.com/oz/politics.html

Australian government and public service management innovation
http://www.innovations.gov.au/

Australian National University politics page
http://www.anu.edu.au/polsci/austpol/aust/aust.html

Malcolm Farnsworth's political resources page
http://netspace.net.au/%7Emalcolm/

Institute of Public Administration Australia
http://www.dowdigital.com.au/ipaa/index.html

Lobby Guide for Australia
http://www.ozemail.com.au/~trc/lgpt1.html

David Moss' politics page
http://www.adfa.oz.au/~adm/politics/

Palmer's Australian Politics page
http://www.pcug.org.au/~bpalmer/

Appendix        145

Commonwealth Parliamentary Library's politics and public administration page
http://par18.aph.gov.au/library/polpubad.htm

## Australian news and current affairs sources

*The Age*
http://www.theage.com.au/

Australian Broadcasting Corporation
http://www.abc.net.au/news

*The Australian*
http://www.australian.aust.com/index.htm

*Australian Financial Review*
http://www.afr.com.au/

*Canberra Times*
http://www.canberratimes.com.au/

F@rming Online
http://www.rpl.com.au/farming/

*Sydney Morning Herald*
http://www.smh.com.au/

## International Internet public policy and politics resources

National governments and international organisations

*Canada*

Official Canadian Government home page
http://canada.gc.ca/

Canada's Parliament — English language entry point
http://www.parl.gc.ca/english/

Canadian Prime Minister's home page
http://pm.gc.ca/

Canadian Supreme Court home page
http://xinfo.ic.gc.ca/opengov/supreme.court/sc.home.html

*Commonwealth of Nations*

Commonwealth Secretariat home page
http://www.thecommonwealth.org/

Commonwealth Liaison Unit of Canada entry point
http://www.comnet.ca/~comquest/

Commonwealth Parliamentary Association
http://www.comparlas.co.uk/HQ/index.htm

The Commonwealth Online
http://www.tcd.co.uk

*European Community*

European Union English language entry point
http://europa.eu.int/index-en.htm

European Parliament English language entry point
http://www.europarl.eu.int/sg/tree/en/default.htm

*New Zealand*

Official New Zealand Government home page
http://www.govt.nz/

New Zealand Parliament home page
http://www.parliament.govt.nz/

New Zealand executive government home page
http://www.executive.govt.nz/

Legal Information Institute of New Zealand
http://www.liinz.org.nz/

*South Africa*

South African Government of National Unity (African National Congress page)
http://www.anc.org.za/gnu/

South African government information from the South African Communication Service
http://www.sacs.org.za/level1/govinfo.htm

South African Constitutional Assembly
http://www.constitution.org.za/

*United Kingdom*

a well structured entry point to UK government
http://www.open.gov.uk/

10 Downing Street
http://www.number-10.gov.uk/index.html

the Head of State for the UK (and Australia)
http://www.royal.gov.uk/

the Houses of Parliament
http://www.parliament.uk/

Her Majesty's Stationery Office
http://www.hmso.gov.uk/

*United Nations*

Official UN home page
http://www.un.org/

links to UN organisations
http://www.unsystem.org/

Global Policy Forum
http://www.igc.apc.org/globalpolicy/

*United States*

the President's residence
http://www.whitehouse.gov/

US House of Representatives
http://www.house.gov/

US Senate
http://www.senate.gov/

US Office of Government Ethics Home Page
http://www.access.gpo.gov/usoge/

Library of Congress list of US Government home pages
http://lcweb.loc.gov/global/executive/fed.html

Yahoo! list of US government department home pages
http://www.yahoo.com/Government/Executive_Branch/Departments_and_Agencies/

## Public policy resources

Brookings Institution
http://www.brook.edu/

*CIA World Factbook*
http://www.odci.gov/cia/publications/nsolo/factbook/global.htm

Conservative Party (UK)
http://www.conservative-party.org.uk/

Electronic Policy Network
http://epn.org/

Hubert H. Humphrey Institute of Public Affairs
http://www.hhh.umn.edu/

Institute of Public Policy
http://ralph.gmu.edu/

*International Public Management Journal*
http://www.willamette.edu/~fthompso/ipmn/research/journal/index.html

Jay's Leftist and Progressive Internet Resources
http://www.neravt.com/left/

J.F. Kennedy School of Government
http://ksgwww.harvard.edu/

Labour Party (UK)
http://www.labour.org.uk/core.html

Labour Related Internet Resources (US)
http://www.lib.berkeley.edu/IIRL/iirlnet.html

Political Intrigue
http://www.cjr.columbia.edu/virtual/trailsb.html

Public Administration, Canada
http://www.dsuper.net/~pdubeau/indexen.html

Turn Left
http://www.cjnetworks.com/~cubsfan/lineral.html

## International news and current affairs sources

*Asia Times*
http://www.asiatimes.com/

*Bangkok Post*, Thailand
http://www.bangkokpost.net/

BBC
http://www.bbc.co.uk/

*China Daily*
http://www.chinadaily.co.cn/cndy/cd_cate1.html

CNN / *Time magazine*
http://allpolitics.com/

*The Economist*, UK
http://www.economist.com/

Editor and Publisher (newspaper links)
http://www.mediainfo.com/ephome/npaper/nphtm/online.htm

*Globe and Mail*, Canada
http://www.theglobeandmail.com/

*The Guardian*, UK
http://go2.guardian.co.uk/

*Hong Kong Standard*
http://www.hkstandard.com/

*Irish Times*, Dublin
http://www.irish-times.com/

*Japan Times*
http://www.japantimes.co.jp/

*Johannesburg Star*, South Africa
http://www.inc.co.za/online/star/

*Manilla Bulletin*, Phillipines
http://www.mb.com.ph/

*Mother Jones Magazine*
http://www.motherjones.com/index.html

*The National*, Papua New Guinea
http://www.wr.com.au/national/home.html

*The Observer* (UK)
http://www.observer.co.uk/

*Papua New Guinea Post-Courier*
http://www.datec.com.au/postcourier/

Appendix

*The Star*, Malaysia
http://www.jaring.my/~star/

*Straits Times*, Singapore
http://straitstimes.asia1.com/

*The Telegraph* (UK)
http://www.telegraph.co.uk/

*Time Magazine* (USA)
http://www.time.com

*The Times*, UK
http://www.the-times.co.uk/

*The Times of India*
http://www.timesofindia.com/

*Toronto Star*
http://www.thestar.com/

*United Nations News*
http://www.un.org/News/

*USA Today*
http://www.usatoday.com/

*Washington Post*, USA
http://www.washingtonpost.com/

# References

Alinsky, S.D. 1971. *Rules for Radicals: A Pragmatic Primer for the Realistic Radical*, New York: Vintage Books.

Anderson, J.E. 1994. *Public Policymaking: an introduction*, 2nd edition, Boston: Houghton Mifflin.

Atkinson, M.M. and Nigol, R.A. 1989. 'Selecting Policy Instruments: neo-institutional and rational choice interpretations of automobile insurance in Ontario', *Canadian Journal of Political Science*, 22, 1:107–35.

Aucoin, P. 1986. 'Organizational Change in the Canadian Machinery of Government: from rational management to brokerage politics', *Canadian Journal of Political Science*, 19, 1:3–27.

Bachrach, P. and Baratz, M.S. 1963. 'Decisions and Nondecisions: an analytical framework', *American Political Science Review*, 57, 3:632–42.

Berlin, I. 1996. 'On Political Judgement', *New York Review of Books*, 3 October, 26–30.

Boston, J., Martin, J., Pallot, J. and Walsh, P. 1996. *Political Management: the New Zealand model*, Auckland: Oxford University Press.

Brewer, G. and deLeon, P. 1983. *The Foundations of Policy Analysis*, Homewood, Ill.: Dorsey Press.

Burch, M. and Wood, B. 1989. *Public Policy in Britain*, Oxford: Blackwell.

Cobb, R.W. and Elder, C.D. 1972. *Participation in American Politics: the dynamics of agenda-building*, Baltimore: Johns Hopkins University Press.

Codd, M. 1990. 'Cabinet Operations of the Australian Government', in B. Galligan, J.R. Nethercote and C. Walsh (eds), *The Cabinet and Budget Process*, Canberra: Centre for Research on Federal Financial Relations, 1–22.

Colebatch, H.K. 1993. 'Policy-Making and Volatility: what is the problem?', in A. Hede and S. Prasser (eds), *Policy-Making in Volatile Times*, Sydney: Hale and Iremonger.

Considine, M. 1994. *Public Policy: a critical approach*, Melbourne: Macmillan.

Corbett, D. 1996. *Australian Public Sector Management*, 2nd edition, Sydney: Allen & Unwin.

Crossfield, L. and Byrne, A. 1994. *Review of the Evaluation Function in DEET*, Department of Employment, Education and Training, Canberra: AGPS.

Cupps, S.D. 1977. 'Emerging Problems of Citizen Participation', *Public Administration Review*, 37, 5:478–487.

Davis, G. 1990. 'The Politics of Traffic Lights: professionals in public bureaucracy', *Australian Journal of Public Administration*, 49, 1:63–74.

Davis, G. 1995. *A Government of Routines: executive coordination in an Australian State*, Melbourne: Macmillan.

Davis, G. 1996. *Consultation, Public Participation, and the Integration of Multiple Interests into Policy Making*, report prepared for the Organisation for Economic Cooperation and Development, Paris, May.

Davis, G., Wanna, J., Warhurst, J. and Weller, P. 1993. *Public Policy in Australia*, 2nd edition, Sydney: Allen & Unwin.

Davis, G. and Weller, P. 1987. 'Negotiated Policy or Metanonsense? A response to the policy prescriptions of Murray Frazer', *Australian Journal of Public Administration*, 46, 4:380–87.

Davis, G. and Weller, P. 1993. *Strategic Management in the Public Sector: managing the coastal zone*, report prepared for the Resources Assessment Commission, Brisbane: Griffith University.

Department of Finance. 1994. *Doing Evaluations: a practical guide*, Canberra: Department of Finance.

Department of Finance. n.d. *Reasons Why Evaluation Should Be Done and Why Finance Should be Involved*, Canberra: Department of Finance.

Department of Premier and Cabinet. 1996. *Cabinet Office*, 26 November, http://www.vic.gov.au/stategov/dpccab.html.

Department of the Prime Minister and Cabinet. 1988. *Cabinet Handbook*, Canberra: AGPS.

Department of the Prime Minister and Cabinet. 1996. *The Role of the Department of the Prime Minister and Cabinet*, 28 March, http://www.nla.gov.au/pmc/pmcrole.html.

Department of the Prime Minister and Cabinet. 1997. *Home Page*, 8 August, http://www.nla.gov.au/pmc/pmchome.html.

Department of Treasury and Finance. 1995. 'Budget Branches', *Department of Treasury and Finance*

Branches, http://dino.slsa.sa.gov.au/sagov/agencies/dtf/dtfbranch.htm.

Dery, D. 1984. *Problem Definition in Policy Analysis*, Lawrence: University of Kansas Press.

Donnison, O. 1994. 'By What Authority? Ethics and Policy Analysis', *Social Policy and Administration*, 28, 1:20–32.

Downs, A. 1972. 'Up and Down with Ecology — the "issue-attention cycle"', *The Public Interest*, 28, Summer, 38–50.

EARC. 1992. *Report on Codes of Conduct for Public Officials*, Brisbane: Electoral and Administrative Review Commission.

Emy, H.V. 1976. *Public Policy: problems and paradoxes*, Melbourne: Macmillan.

Emy, H.V. and Hughes, O. 1991. *Australian Politics: realities in conflict*, 2nd edition, Melbourne: Macmillan.

Eyestone, R. 1978. *From Social Issues to Public Policy*, New York: Wiley.

Fischer, F. 1995. *Evaluating Public Policy*, Chicago: Nelson-Hall.

Fitzgerald, T. 1989. *Report of a Commission of Inquiry Pursuant to Orders in Council*, Brisbane: Government Printer.

Franklin, N.E. 1992. 'Initiative and Referendum: participatory democracy or rolling back the state?' in M. Munro-Clark (ed), *Citizen Participation in Government*, Sydney: Hale and Iremonger, 55–68.

Gore, A. 1993. *Creating A Government That Works Better and Costs Less: the Gore report on reinventing government*, New York: Times Books (a commercial publication of the report of the National Performance Review).

Guba, E.G. and Lincoln, Y.S. 1987. *Effective Evaluation*, San Francisco: Jossey-Bass.

Guba, E.G. and Lincoln, Y.S. 1989. *Fourth Generation Evaluation*, Newbury Park: Sage.

Gunn, L.A. 1978. 'Why is Implementation so Difficult?', *Management Services in Government*, 33:169–76.

Hasluck, P. 1968. *The Public Servant and Politics*, Robert Garran Memorial Oration, Canberra: Royal Institution of Public Administration Australia.

Hayes, M.T. 1992. *Incrementalism and Public Policy*, New York: Longman.

Hogwood, B.W. and Gunn, L.A. 1990. *Policy Analysis for the Real World*, Oxford: Oxford University Press.

Hood, C.C. 1983. *The Tools of Government*, London: Macmillan.

Holden, A. and O'Faircheallaigh, C. 1995. *Economic and Social Impact of Silica Mining at Cape Flattery*, Aboriginal Politics and Public Sector Management, Research Monograph No. 1, Brisbane: Centre for Australian Public Sector Management, Griffith University, November.

Howard, J. 1996. *A Guide on Key Elements of Ministerial Responsibility*, Canberra: Department of the Prime Minister and Cabinet, April.

Howlett, M. 1991. 'Policy Instruments, Policy Styles, and Policy Implementation: national approaches to theories of instrument choice', *Policy Studies Journal*, 19, 2:1–21.

Howlett, M. and Ramesh, M. 1995. *Studying Public Policy: policy cycles and policy subsystems*, Don Mills, Ontario: Oxford University Press.

Ingram, H. 1990. 'Implementation: a review and suggested framework', in N.B. Lynn and A. Wildavsky (eds), *Public Administration: the state of the discipline*, New Jersey: Chatham House.

Jones, T. 1997. 'Diary', *London Review of Books*, 5 June, 37.

Keating, M. 1996. 'Defining the Policy Advising Function', in J. Uhr and K. Mackay (eds), *Evaluating Policy Advice*, Canberra: Federalism Research Centre and the Department of Finance, 61–67.

Kettner, P.M. and Martin, L.L. 1987. *Purchase of Service Contracting: a Sage human services guide*, Newbury Park: Sage.

Kingdon, J. 1995. *Agendas, Alternatives, and Public Policies*, 2nd edition, New York: Harper Collins.

Lasswell, H. 1951. 'The Policy Orientation', in D. Lerner and H. Lasswell (eds), *The Policy Sciences*, Stanford: Stanford University Press.

Lindblom, C.E. 1959. 'The Science of "Muddling Through"', *Public Administration Review*, 19, 2:79–88.

Lindblom, C.E. 1965. *The Intelligence of Democracy*, New York: Free Press.

Lindblom, C.E. 1979. *Politics and Markets*, New York: Basic Books.

Lindblom, C.E. 1980. *The Policy-Making Process*, 2nd edition, New Jersey: Prentice-Hall.

Linder, S.H. and Peters, B.G. 1989. 'Instruments of Government: perceptions and contexts', *Journal of Public Policy*, 9, 1:35–58.

Lunde, T.K. 1996. 'Client Consultation and Participation: consumers and public services', in OECD, *Responsive Government: service quality initiatives*, PUMA Public Management Service, OECD, Paris, 71–83.

MAB-MIAC. 1992. *The Australian Public Service Reformed: an evaluation of the decade of management reform*, Taskforce on Management Improvement Prepared for the Commonwealth Government Management Advisory Board with Guidance from the Management Improvement Advisory Committee, Canberra: AGPS.

Machiavelli, N. [1513] 1988. *The Prince* (ed. Q. Skinner and R. Price), Cambridge: Cambridge University Press.

MacIntyre, A. 1983. 'The Indispensability of Political Theory', in D. Miller and L. Siedentop (eds), *The Nature of Political Theory*, Oxford: Clarendon Press.

Mackay, K. 1996. *The Institutional Framework for Evaluation in the Australian Government*, paper presented to a World Bank Seminar on Australia's Program and Policy Evaluation Framework, Washington DC, 30 April.

Majone, G. and Wildavsky, A. 1979. 'Implementation as Evolution', in A. Pressman and A. Wildavsky (eds), *Implementation*, 3rd edition, Berkeley: University of California Press.

March, J. and Olsen, J. 1989, *Rediscovering Institutions: The Organisational Basis of Politics*, New York: Free Press.

Miser, H.J. and Quade, E.S. 1988. 'Toward Quality Control', in H.J. Miser and E.S. Quade (eds) *Handbook of Systems Analysis: craft issues and procedural choices*, Chichester: Wiley.

Muller, D. and Headey, B. 1996. 'Agenda-Setters and Policy Influentials: results from the Victoria agendas project', *Australian Journal of Political Science*, 31, 2:135–52.

Munro-Clarke, M. (ed.). 1992. *Citizen Participation in Government*, Sydney: Hale and Iremonger.

OECD, 1994. *Country Study on Public Consultation: Canada*, paper prepared for the Meeting on Public Consultation in Regulatory Development, Paris, August.

OECD 1994a. *Public Consultation in Regulatory Development: practices and experiences in ten OECD countries*, paper prepared for the PUMA OECD Meeting on Public Consultation in Regulatory Development, Paris, October.

OECD, 1996. *Responsive Government: service quality initiatives*, PUMA, Organisation for Economic Co-operation and Development, Paris.

OECD, 1997. *Managing Government Ethics*, PUMA Public Management Service, Organisation for Economic Co-operation and Development, Paris, February.

Office of the Cabinet, 1992. *Queensland Cabinet Handbook*, Brisbane: Goprint.

Office of the Cabinet, 1993. *Consultation: a resource document for the Queensland public sector*, Brisbane: Goprint.

Office of the Cabinet, 1995. *Queensland Cabinet Handbook*, 2nd edition, Brisbane: Goprint.

Office of the Cabinet, 1996. *Queensland Policy Handbook*, Brisbane: Goprint.

Painter, M. 1981. 'Central Agencies and the Coordination Principle', *Australian Journal of Public Administration*, 40, 4:265–80.

Painter, M. 1987. *Steering the Modern State: changes in central coordination in three Australian State governments*, Sydney: University of Sydney Press.

Painter, M. 1992. 'Participation and Power', in M. Munro-Clarke (ed.), 21–36.

Patton, C.V. and Sawicki, D.S. 1993. *Basic Methods of Policy Analysis and Planning*, 2nd edition, New Jersey: Prentice Hall.

Pressman, J. and Wildavsky, A. 1973. *Implementation: how great expectations in Washington are dashed in Oakland; or, why it's amazing that federal programs work at all, this being a saga of the Economic Development Administration as told by two sympathetic observers who seek to build morals on a foundation of ruined hopes*, Berkeley: University of California Press.

PSMC. 1993. *Policy Development and Advice*, Executive Development Program, Senior Executive Service, Public Sector Management Commission (John Wanna et al.), kits 1–4, Brisbane: PSMC.

Public Service and Merit Protection Commission. 1996. *About our Values, Mission, Role and Goals*, 19 March, http://www.psmpc.gov.au/about/mission.htm.

Putnam, R.D. 1995. 'Tuning In, Tuning Out: the strange disappearance of social capital in America', *PS: Political Science and Politics*, 2, 4:664–83.

Quade, E.S. 1982. *Analysis for Public Decisions*, 2nd edition, New York: North Holland.

Republican Advisory Committee. 1993. *The Options — the Report*, The Report of the Republican Advisory Committee, Canberra: AGPS.

Rittel, H.W.J. and Weber, M.W. 1973. 'Dilemmas in a General Theory of Planning', *Policy Sciences*, 4:155–69.

Sabatier, P. 1982. 'Regulating Coastal Land Use in California, 1973–75', *Policy Studies Journal*, 11: 88–102.

Sabatier, P. 1986. 'Top-Down and Bottom-Up Approaches to Implementation Research', *Journal of Public Policy*, 6:21–48.

Sabatier, P. 1988. 'An Advocacy Coalition Framework of Policy Change and the Role of Policy-Orientated Learning Therein', *Policy Sciences*, 21:129–69.

Sabatier, P.A. and Jenkins-Smith, H.C. (eds) 1993. *Policy Change and Learning*, Boulder: Westview Press.

Scales, B. 1997. 'Performance Monitoring Public Services in Australia', *Australian Journal of Public Administration*, 56, 1:100–109.

Schattschneider, E.E. 1960. *The Semi-Sovereign People*, New York: Holt, Rinehart and Winston.

Schneider, A and Ingram, H. 1988. 'Systematically Pinching Ideas: a comparative approach to public policy', *Journal of Public Policy*, 8, 1:61–80.

Shand, D. and Arnberg, M. 1996. 'Background Paper', in OECD, *Responsive Government*, PUMA Public Management Service, OECD, Paris, 15–38.

Sharkansky, I. 1970. *The Routines of Politics*, New York: Van Nostrand Reinhold.

Shergold, P. 1997. 'Ethics and the Changing Nature of Public Service', *Australian Journal of Public Administration*, 56, 1:119–24.

Simeon, R. 1976. 'Studying Public Policy', *Canadian Journal of Public Administration*, 9, 4:540–80.

Simon, H.A. 1973. 'The Structure of Ill-Structured Problems', *Artificial Intelligence*, 4:181–201.

Sturgess, G. 1996. 'Virtual Government: what will remain inside the public sector?', *Australian Journal of Public Administration*, 55, 3:59–73.

Taylor, J. 1993. Interpreting Disorder Within a Transaction Cost Framework: a case study of the delivery of early intervention services in three Australian States, doctoral dissertation, Griffith University.

Thomas, J.C. 1990. 'Public Involvement in Public Management: adapting and testing a borrowed theory', *Public Administration Review*, 50, 4:435–445.

Thomas, J.C. 1993. 'Public Involvement and Governmental Effectiveness: a decision-making model for public managers', *Administrative Science and Society*, 24, 4:444–69.

Uhr, J. and Mackay, K. (eds) 1996. *Evaluating Policy Advice: learning from Commonwealth experience*, Canberra: Federalism Research Centre and the Department of Finance.

Waller, M. 1996. 'Framework for Policy Evaluation', in J. Uhr and K. Mackay (eds), *Evaluating Policy Advice*, Canberra: Federalism Research Centre and the Department of Finance, 9–20.

Walter, J. 1992. 'Prime Ministers and their Staff', in P. Weller (ed), *From Menzies to Keating: the development of the Australian prime ministership*, Carlton: Melbourne University Press, 28–63.

Wanna, J., O'Faircheallaigh, C. and Weller, P. 1992. *Public Sector Management in Australia*, Melbourne: Macmillan.

Wanna, J., Davis, G., Weller, P. and Robinson, M. 1994. *Policy Development and Advice: executive development program*, Senior Executive Service, Brisbane: Public Sector Management Commission.

Ward, I. 1995. *Politics of the Media*, Melbourne: Macmillan.

Weimar, D.L. and Vining, A.R. 1992. *Policy Analysis: concepts and practice*, 2nd edition, Englewood Cliffs: Prentice Hall.

Weller, P. 1990. 'Cabinet and the Prime Minister', in J. Summers, D. Woodward and A. Parkin (eds), *Government, Politics and Power in Australia*, 4th edition, Melbourne: Longman Cheshire, 28–42.

Weller, P. 1992. 'Prime Ministers and Cabinet', in P. Weller (ed.) *Menzies to Keating: the development of the Australian prime ministership*, Melbourne University Press, 5–27.

Weller, P. (ed) 1994. *Royal Commissions and the Making of Public Policy*, Melbourne: Macmillan.

Weller, P. and Grattan, M. 1981. *Can Ministers Cope? Australian federal ministers at work*, Melbourne: Hutchinson.

Wildavsky, A. 1973. 'If Planning is Everything, Maybe it's Nothing', *Policy Sciences* 4:127–53.

Wildavsky, A. 1987. *Speaking Truth to Power: the art and craft of policy analysis*, New Brunswick: Transaction Books.

# Index

Aboriginal and Torres Strait Islander Commission 71, 85, 102
abortion 73
accountability 11, 19
administrative law 11
Alinsky, S. 39
American system of government 8, 10, 17, 73
Anderson, J. 21, 35, 50, 106, 111, 118
*Anti-discrimination Act* 64
anti-smoking campaigns 61, 88
Arnberg, M. 67
assessment studies 72
Atkinson, M. 59, 60
Aucoin, P. 15
Australian Agency for International Development 86
Australian Aid Abroad 109
Australian Broadcasting Corporation 108
Australian Business Council 71
Australian Constitution 8, 10, 53, 60, 68, 92, 99
Australian Council of Social Service 71
Australian Medical Association 61
Australian National Line 108
Australian system of government (*see also responsible government*) 8, 92
Australian Taxation Office 86, 102
Australian Vice-Chancellors' Committee (AV-CC) 101
*Authority to Introduce/Prepare* submission 95

Bachrach, P. 38
Baratz, M.S. 38
Berlin, I. 43
biodiversity 53
Brewer, G. 44, 45
briefing paper 25, 27, 48, 118
budgets 16, 18, 22, 63, 84, 91
Burch, M. 22, 23
Byrne, A. 116

cabinet (*see also executive*) 5, 9, 13, 15, 28, 32, 34, 63, 77, 79, 82, 88, 90–100, 103, 105–106, 110, 114, 120, 122, 127
   agenda 10, 31, 33, 90, 93
   committees 95
   decisions 98–100
   handbook 14, 84–87, 91–92, 94–95, 101, 114, 120–21

   minutes 92, 98–99, 105
   office 81–82, 86, 92
   policy unit 17, 97
   roles of 10
   secrecy 93
   secretary/secretariat 92–93, 97–99
   submission 14, 19, 26, 78–80, 84, 90–95, 97–98, 101, 103, 105, 107, 121, 124, 126, 128
   weekly cycle of 18
Canada 76
Capital Duplicators 33
cause and effect 5, 6, 111
central agencies 14, 16–17, 27, 45, 78–82, 84–85, 88–89, 91, 120–21, 127–28, 131
chief minister (*see prime minister*)
citizen initiated referenda 73
Cobb, R. 34–35
Codd, M. 95, 122
Colebatch, H. 3–4
committee
   interdepartmental 26
   reports 95
   system 9, 59
Commonwealth Bank 108
community groups (*see interest groups*)
competitive neutrality and commercialisation 51
competitive service delivery 51
Considine, M. 25, 75
constitution (*see Australian Constitution*)
Coombs inquiry 71
Corbett, D. 117, 122
cost-benefit analysis 50, 56, 67
cost-effective analysis 50, 56
Council of Australian Governments (COAG) 79, 96, 102
courts (*see judiciary*)
critical path method 125–26
Crossfield, L. 116

daylight saving 69
delegation 72, 74
deLeon, P. 44, 45
democracy 66
departmental policy groups 87
departmentalisation 81
departments 42, 46, 78
   Attorney-General 84
   Education 109

Employment, Education, Training and Youth Affairs 85, 101–102, 116
Environment, Sports and Territories 86, 88
Finance 16, 18, 27–28, 83–84, 102, 112–15, 124
Foreign Affairs and Trade 86, 131
Health 61
Primary Industries 88
the Prime Minister and Cabinet (PM&C) 14, 17, 27–28, 47, 80–81, 85, 95–99, 128
Transport 27–28
Treasury 16, 18, 80, 83–84, 86, 128
Treasury and Finance (SA) 84
Dery, D. 40
direct democracy 72
Donnison, D. 131
Downs, A. 35
due process 78

early intervention program for children with intellectual disabilities 25, 45
ecological sustainability 53
Elder, C. 34, 35
elections 8, 22, 65
Electoral and Administrative Review Commission 123
Emy, H. 9, 130
environment policy 23, 71, 116
environmental impact study 53, 72
ethics 122–23
Ethnic Communities Council 60
euthanasia 73
executive (*see also cabinet*) 4, 8–11
executive council 9, 96, 99
    handbook 99
    minutes 96, 99
Expenditure Review Committee 16
extended trading hours 69
Eyestone, R. 34

Fisher, F. 113, 115, 118, 131
fisheries management 68
Fitzgerald inquiry 71
Fitzgerald, T. 123
focus group research 69
Forster, J. 70
Franklin, N. 71
freedom of information legislation 64

Galbraith, J.K. 87

Gantt chart 125
Gore, A. 129
government
    administration of 11–12, 14, 18
    coordination 17
    functional approach to 12
    parallel processing 29
    routines 2, 18–20, 77, 79, 91, 100, 130, 132–33
governor (*see governor-general*)
governor-general 8–10, 96, 99
Gratton, M. 15, 123
green paper 70
Guba, E.G. 119
Gunn, L. 6, 104

habitat preservation 53
Hasluck, Sir Paul 20
Hawke, Bob 15
Hayes, M.T. 46, 55
Headley, B. 36
Health Consumers Forum 71
Heart Foundation 61
High Court (*see judiciary*)
Higher Education Contribution Scheme (HECS) 101
Hogwood, B. 6
Holden, A. 72
Hood, C.C. 59, 60, 65
House of Commons 8
House of Representatives 9
Howard Government 5, 32
Howard, John 10, 11, 15, 17, 92, 94–97, 99
Howlett, M. 59, 104
Hughes, O. 9
Human Rights and Equal Opportunity Commission 64

*Income Tax Assessment Act* 64
incrementalism 54–56
individual rights 53
industrial relations 32
Industry Commission 71
Ingram, H. 41, 104
Institute of Public Administration Australia 130
interest groups 1, 15, 23, 25, 27–28, 30–35, 44, 68, 70, 75, 78, 127
Internet 32, 142–48
issue attention cycle 35–36
issue drivers 31
    external 32–34
issue identification 36–38, 39

Jenkins-Smith, H. 21–23, 71
Johnson, Lyndon 16, 47
Jones, T. 119
judiciary 9–11, 32–33, 60, 64, 108

Keating, M. 26, 47, 78, 79, 92
Keating, Paul 128
Kennedy, John F. 88
Kennett, Jeff 16
Kettner, P.M. 116
Kingdon, J. 32, 36–37
Krumholtz, N. 70

Laswell, H. 21
legislation submissions 95
*Legislative Standards Act* 54
legislature (*see parliament*)
Lincoln, Y.S. 119
Lindblom, C. 54–56, 107, 110
Linder, S.H. 107
local government 60–64, 79

McAlpine, A. 34
Machiavelli, N. 124
Mackay, K. 113
Majone, G. 111
Mansfield inquiry 71
March, J. 18
Martin, L.L. 116
marijuana 59
*Matters without Submission* 96
media 1, 18, 24, 27–28, 30–31, 35–36, 44
mega-departments 131
minister 1, 9, 11–16, 20, 31–32, 44, 46–48, 87, 91–92, 94–95, 97, 100, 111, 114, 120, 123, 128, 132
    assisting the prime minister for public service 85
    attorney-general 97
    finance 97
    industrial relations 97
ministerial advisers (*see political advisers*)
ministerial coordinating committees 79
ministerial responsibility 93
monetary policy 68
moral issues 72
Muller, D. 36

national competition policy (NCP) 51
National Farmers' Federation 71
National Union of Students (NUS) 101
*Native Title Act* 33

natural resource management 53
New York stock market 33
New Zealand 73
Newman, D. 13
Nigol, R. 59, 60
non-decisions 38

OECD 67, 71, 73, 76
Office of the Cabinet (*see also Department of the Prime Minister and Cabinet*) 74, 94, 98
O'Faircheallaigh, C. 72
Olsen, J. 18
opinion polls 75
opportunity cost 50

Painter, M. 72, 78
parliament 1, 8–11, 13–14, 30–31, 35, 53, 63, 73, 127
    Queensland 54, 74
Parliamentary Counsel 84
Patton, C.V. 109
peak bodies 71
performance indicators 91, 118
Peters, B.G. 107
policy learning process 111
political advisers 13, 18–19, 35, 111, 128
political parties 30–31, 36
poll tax 58
premier (*see prime minister*)
prime minister 9, 11, 13, 15–18, 32, 78, 80, 82, 92, 95, 97–98, 121–22
    chief of staff 17
private health insurance 5
privatisation 108
Pressman, J. 104, 105, 110
pressure groups (*see interest groups*)
problem solving
    scientific approach to 42
problems
    ill-structured 37
    well-structured 37
    wicked 37–38, 47, 65
procedural integrity 2, 121
Productivity Commission 86
professional neutrality 8
prostitution 72
public hearings/inquiries 68, 70–72
public information campaign 69
public meetings 75
public policy
    advice 11, 46

Index 155

agenda 30–31, 35–36, 40, 96
analysis 6, 14, 24–25, 41–57, 127
    as authoritative choice 4
    as hypothesis 5–6
    as objective 6
consultation 14, 24–25, 66–76, 91, 124, 127
coordination 14, 24–25, 77–89, 91, 105, 127, 131
cycle 1–2, 6, 12, 14, 18, 21–32, 35, 40, 43–44, 58, 66, 72, 90–91, 94, 103, 105, 111–13, 118, 122–27, 131–32
decision 24, 26, 90–100, 127
definition of 3
evaluation 6, 14, 19, 24, 26, 105, 112–19, 127
failure 108–11, 124
implementation 6, 14, 24, 26, 103–111, 124, 127
instruments 24–25, 58–65, 105–106, 127
issue identification 24, 30–40, 127
liaison units 87
objectives 45–46
proposals 14
target group 106
vs private policy 5
public servants 1, 8, 10–12, 15, 19, 26, 66, 96, 98, 100, 108–109, 128, 132
public service 13–15, 20, 34, 92, 111
    career 9
    employment 16
    non-partisan 16
    reductions 32
Public Service and Merit Protection Commission 85

Qantas 108
Quade, E. 44

Ramesh, M. 59, 104
rational comprehensive model 42–43, 54–55
reduced outlays 51
referendum 68–69, 72–73
regulatory impact 51
Republic Advisory Committee 10
Reserve Bank 68
responsible government 8–9, 11–12, 34
    traditional model 19
Rittel, H.W.J. 38
routines (*see government routines*)

Sabatier, P. 21, 22, 23, 71, 105, 111
same-sex relationships 73
Sawicki, D.S. 109
Scales, B. 116

Schneider, A. 41
Senate 8, 31
senior executive service 17
service delivery 11
Shand, D. 67
Sharkansky, I. 19
Shergold, P. 121
*Significant Appointments* 96
Simeon, R. 22–23
Simon, H. 37
social impact studies 72
social justice principles 52
Solicitor-General 84
statutory authorities 78
strategic plans 19, 91
Sturgess, G. 63
surveys 68–69
Sydney airport 27–28, 59

talk-back radio 75
tax policy 62
Taylor, J. 44–45, 109
10 day rule 18, 93
territory administrator (*see governor-general*)
Thatcher, Margaret 58
think tanks 32, 128
Thomas, J. 68
treasurer 16, 79, 97
Treasurer's Reserve 84

Uhr, J. 113, 122
unions 1, 68, 71
universities 108

Victoria 82
Vietnam war 47
Vining, A.R. 50

Waller, M. 57, 113
Walter, J. 14
Wanna, J. 16, 56, 77, 80, 91, 128
Ward, I. 34
Webber, M.W. 38
Weimar, D.L. 50
Weller, P. 10, 11, 12, 15, 29, 72, 104, 123
whole of government approach 78, 85, 97, 131
Wildavsky, A. 6, 41, 45, 80, 86, 104, 105, 110–11
Wilson, Harold 18, 38, 72
Wood, B. 22, 23
woodchip exports 88

## OTHER RECENT BOOKS FROM ALLEN & UNWIN

## Accountability and Corruption
*Public sector ethics*

**Edited by Gordon L. Clark, Elizabeth Prior Jonson and Wayne Caldow**

*Public sector ethics* is in the limelight. The issue is simple: corrupt public officials should be exposed, prosecuted and gaoled, just like their colleagues in the private sector. Thus we have had inquiries into the conduct of state governments, departments including the police, and elected officials including state premiers.

This book is about public sector ethics; the practice of government; the relations between officials, their advisers and the public; as well as the interplay between politics and statecraft.

1 86448 423 3

## Australian Public Sector Management
*Second edition*

**David Corbett**

*Australian Public Sector Management* is designed as a textbook, although its highly readable style and appreciation of the practical issues makes it a standard for the public sector manager. Blending theory and practice, David Corbett covers the critical problems facing the public sector in the age of corporatisation and privatisation. After introducing the framework of and stakeholders in government, he explores strategic planning and budgeting, guiding and managing people, accountability and ethics, performance evaluation and decision-making theory.

This new second edition offers new chapters on privatisation, regulation and the increasingly important issue of international public sector cooperation and structures.

1 86448 160 9

# New Ideas, Better Government

## Edited by Patrick Weller and Glyn Davis

The quest for better public sector management is worldwide. Every country is exploring ways of providing services better and more efficiently—ways of reinventing government.

Learning from one another is an obvious strategy for governments intent on reform. *New Ideas, Better Government* enables lessons to be drawn from comparative experiences. By examining the reform strategies of governments in Australia, the United States, Britain and New Zealand, and by comparing or analysing their impact, the authors provide insights into the process and lessons on what does, or does not, work

The result is stimulating and provocative, and will encourage readers to assess the impact of the reform agenda, challenging their assumptions about the best ways to introduce reform.

1 86448 014 9

# The Great Experiment

*Labour parties and public policy transfers in Australia and New Zealand*

## Francis Castles, Rolf Gerritsen and Jack Vowles

Labour parties came to power in Australia in 1983 and in New Zealand in 1984. In both countries, the new governments embarked on programs of economic and social transformation more comprehensive in scope and intensity than elsewhere in the Western world.

This book examines how public policies have been transformed in Australia and New Zealand, the contrasts between the two nations and the likely consequences for politics and future policy directions.

1 86448 003 3

# Making Social Policy in Australia
*An introduction*

**Tony Dalton, Mary Draper, Wendy Weeks and John Wiseman**

Social policy affects everyone and is everyone's business. Even if you don't receive welfare payments, directly or indirectly you benefit from government services and funding. Yet how are policies and programs actually developed? Can social policy help us create a more just society?

*Making Social Policy in Australia* is a broad introduction to the theory and practice of social policy-making in Australia. The authors explore the history of social policy in Australia, its relationship with economics and other government policy and the policy process. It also reveals the interplay between organisations and the power relations involved.

*Making Social Policy in Australia* is the most up-to-date introduction to Australian social policy currently available, and is essential reading for students and practitioners in human and community service work and government.

1 86448 023 8

# Public Policy in Australia
*Second edition*

**Glyn Davis, John Wanna, John Warhurst and Patrick Weller**

Is Australian public policy unique? Does federalism, an active state system, the structure of government, and the political roles of industry and pressure groups create processes and outcomes different from those of other countries?

By skilfully interweaving theories of governing and decision-making with analysis of Australian policy fields, *Public Policy in Australia* addresses these questions and provides an insightful introduction to public policy.

Designed for undergraduate and masters courses, *Public Policy in Australia* is essential reading for students of public policy, political science, public administration and applied economics.

1 86373 433 3